# THE PROPHETIC SONG

## by

## LaMar Boschman

# The Prophetic Song

**The Worship Institute**
a division of
LaMar Boschman Ministries
P.O. Box 130
Bedford, TX 76095


ISBN: 1-883092-01-9
(previously ISBN 0-938612-12-3)

Printed in U.S.A.

| Fifth Printing: | 1992 | Seventh Printing: | 1995 |
| Sixth Printing: | 1992 | Eighth Printing: | 1999 |

*Inside the U.S.A. call toll free to order:*
**1-800-627-0923**

# Dedication

To Menno and Evelyn Boschman, my parents who raised me to know and obey the Lord Jesus Christ—two very special people whom I love and respect.

# Acknowledgments

I greatly appreciate the skillful contribution Cheryl Tippon has made to this book. Without her tasteful expertise this book would not have been half of what it is. Thank you Cheryl, you are a blessing. You have a gift from God.

Bob Vande Brake, without your positive vision and keen perception this book may have not seen completion. Thank you for your constant assistance.

# Contents

# Foreword

In writing to the Church at Ephesus, Paul directed them to ''be filled with the Spirit; speaking to yourselves in psalms and hymns and spiritual songs, singing and making melody in your heart to the Lord'' (Ephesians 5:18,19), thereby teaching us that the person who is filled with the Spirit will overflow melodiously. He instructed the Colossians, ''Let the word of Christ dwell in you richly in all wisdom; teaching and admonishing one another in psalms and hymns and spiritual songs, singing with grace in your hearts to the Lord'' (Colossians 3:16), which suggests that being full of the Word will also produce a melodious overflow. Obviously, the Holy Spirit is a singing Spirit.

If being full of the Spirit and of the Word finds its highest expression in music, wouldn't it be entirely natural for the prophetic expression of the heart of God to be released melodically? This certainly was true in the life of David, and we have strong indication that it was true in the lives of many others who were used of God in speaking on His behalf.

When we are confronted with the majesty, beauty, magnificence, and love of God, mere verbal expression seems impotent, for often

i

the feeling is as important as the facts, and words are clumsy tools for the expression of feeling; music expresses emotion far better than words do. If we can get the correct words properly wedded to companionate music, both the message and the ecstasy communicate to the listener.

Many of us have been in public services in which we witnessed the proclamation of a prophetic message that was shouted by a speaker who went through great physical gyrations while he spoke. It is unlikely that God needed to shout and flail the arms of the speaker to keep our attention. What is far more likely is that the speaker was overwhelmed with the emotion of God choosing to speak through him, and he did not know how to express that emotion in a manner that would better represent Christ. If only he had known how to release both the fervor and the communication in song, the message would have been far easier to receive.

Most of us are limited in our training, so we never rise above what we have seen others do. LaMar Boschman has sought to enlarge our concepts of what the prophetic word is and how it can be expressed at various levels of inspiration by removing some of the mystery that seems to surround "singing in the Spirit." It has been my joy to offer some assistance to him in the writing of this book, and I am confident that it will become a textbook for many who aspire to minister both unto God and for God. As Aquila and Priscilla took Apollos aside and "explained to him the way of God more accurately" (Acts 18:26, NKJV), so Brother Boschman, in this book, would like to take you aside and explain prophetic utterance more accurately. Give him that chance.

Judson Cornwall, Th.D.

Decatur, GA
June 1986

# Chapter 1
# "And Spiritual Songs"

"O sing unto the LORD a new song: sing unto the LORD, all the earth" (Psalm 96:1)!

When the worship leader began to lead us in the first song of the morning I knew this was going to be an unusual service for me. The air seemed to be filled with anticipation as if the spirit world was on red alert. The songs were exciting and the congregation was turned on to worshipping Jesus. The accordian, piano, tambourine, and trumpet supported the vocal praise.

From this small congregation in Calgary, Canada, the sound of many waters was effecting this young Canadian as I stood among this congregation and worshipped. About a half hour into the worship service I began to sing spontaneous lyrics to any melody that came to my spirit. As fast as it came I sung it. I did not know what was happening and didn't think much of it because everyone else was as much lost in vocal worship as I was.

Several minutes later I realized I was singing a song that had a structure. While I had been worshipping a melody and chord pattern had evolved that resembled a written song. Even the lyrics were in proper meter. I was excited because I knew another prophetic song had been birthed. The tremendous revelation of Jesus that I sensed in the worship caused the song to be birthed.

When the worship of the congregation had quieted I didn't hesitate to lift up my voice and sing it out.

The Lord reigneth, the Lord reigneth,
Blessed be the name of the Lord,
For the Lord our God
Om-ni-po-tent
Reigneth in majesty.

I sang it over and over until the congregation picked it up and together we declared that God reigned. It brought a definite lift to the already powerful service. The prophetic song is a direct result of the revelation of Jesus in the worship service.

This is the hour of singing in the Church of Jesus Christ. This is a day when the Spirit of God is moving upon His people to "sing a new song" unto the Lord. This is a time when we are hearing more and more about "the song of the Lord."

But what is the song of the Lord? Is it a song we sing about the Lord? Is it a song we sing to the Lord? Could it be a song the Lord Himself sings? Where did this song originate? Why do we sing it? How do we sing it? These are only a few of the questions that come to mind when one first hears about "the song of the Lord."

Because these questions arise so frequently, and because the answers to them can help people enter into a new realm of worship, I have set out to write this book. All over the world people are singing the song of the Lord in their worship. Yet there are still many who do not understand it, or perhaps are not even aware that there is such a thing and that God desires it to be a part of their own personal worship experience. This book is for those people, and my prayer and desire is that as they see what God says, they will enter into what He desires.

## "The Song" Defined

The expression "the song of the Lord" is an interesting phrase. Obviously it involves music, but is this a song from God, or is it a song God sings? Both are correct. Just as the term "children of the Lord" delineates both that we come from God and that we are His possession, so the term "song of the Lord" tells us that the song comes from God and that it is His song. We find this expression used in the Scriptural account of the cleansing of the Temple by Hezekiah and the restoration of Temple worship: "And he [Hezekiah] set the Levites in the house of the LORD...for so was the commandment of the LORD by his prophets. And the Levites stood with the instruments of David, and the priests with the trumpets. And Hezekiah commanded to offer the burnt offering upon the altar. And when the burnt offering began, the song of the LORD began also with the trumpets, and with the instruments ordained by David king of Israel. And all the congregation worshipped..."(2 Chronicles 29:25-28). Where there was worship, there was also the song of the Lord.

Paul exhorted the believers to "be filled with the Spirit; speaking to yourselves in psalms and hymns and spiritual songs" (Ephesians 5:18,19), "teaching and admonishing one another in psalms and hymns and spiritual songs" (Colossians 3:16). "Spiritual songs" are songs sung in or by the Holy Spirit. The Greek phrase is *'ode pneumatikos*, meaning songs of the *pneuma*—the breath of God. It could be said that God "exhales" songs through the yielded singer. God inspires and writes songs; He is the great Author and Composer. He gives spontaneous songs of praise and exhortation. These are songs of the Spirit of God.

In this book I will be using the term "the prophetic song" when speaking of what we commonly call "the song of the Lord." As we have just said, this utterance is inspired by the Holy Spirit and is received spontaneously from the Lord. We could say that there

3

is singing **about** the Lord, singing **to** the Lord, and singing **of** the Lord. These are progressively higher expressions of the inspiration of the Holy Spirit within the believer.

At its highest, most of anointed praise and singing is either praise of God or exhortation to men. This is good and necessary but is not equal to God speaking to His people, for the Bible tells us that God can communicate with us at a much higher level. But there is a touch of the prophetic in Spirit-inspired singing. For example, I may be singing to the Lord in praise or worship, exalting His nature or singing His Word, and feel quickened by the Spirit to bring that forth for everyone to hear as a means of exhortation, edification, or comfort. This is not the same as prophecy which flows out of the office of a prophet (as we will explain further in a later chapter), but it is a very elementary level of prophecy. The prophetic song builds up those present; it encourages and brings comfort to the saints.

**Purposes for the Prophetic Song**

Examples of the "song of the Lord" are found throughout the Bible, but in the Psalms we especially see the very patterns of that song. Some commentators choose to divide them according to the Davidic assignment that was given when David brought the Ark back to Jerusalem and set it in the tent that he had prepared for it, for "he appointed certain of the Levites to minister before the ark of the LORD, and to record, and to thank and praise the LORD God of Israel" (1 Chronicles 16:4). The Psalms fit beautifully into these three categories, so it is likely that any prophetic song that flows during our worship times will also fit in one of them.

The New King James Version translates the word "record" as "commemorate"—David "appointed...Levites...to **commemorate**." The Hebrew word is *zakar*, which means "to put in remembrance; to cause to be recorded." Sometimes this commem-

4

oration song was a celebration of a great event or a great person, and at other times it was of historic significance, for much history was recorded in songs in the days before reading and writing were so common. Psalm 78 is Asaph's record of the history of Israel from Egypt to the Promised Land, and in singing it Israel was given a review of her history. It is not unusual or uncommon for the Spirit to sing through a person a song that recounts God's gracious dealings on behalf of that congregation, and that review will bring forth a response of thanksgiving or praise.

This word *zakar* is given as "invoke" in the Revised Standard Version. Commemorative Psalms or songs do tend to invoke in us, or prod us to, expressions of worship toward God. Sometimes when a congregation comes together to worship, the people's minds are so tied up in the happenings of the day that they can't seem to rise above their negative feelings or natural thoughts and praise the Lord. When a musician is inspired of the Spirit to sing a song telling of God's goodness, the attention of the people is drawn from self to God, and praise is a natural result of seeing His goodness, especially if the song calls for a praise response.

Other writers, however, translate the word *zakar* as "to lament." The cry "How shall we sing the LORD'S song in a strange land?" (Psalm 137:4) is the heart of this psalm of lamentation. Captivity had cost these people their songs of joy so that they had nothing left but songs of supplication and lamentation.

In a worshipping congregation it is to be expected that some of the songs which come forth will be individual songs addressed directly to God, petitioning Him to rescue or defend someone. There may also be occasions when the Spirit will quicken a song of general or communal lamentation in which the Church or the nation is lamenting its condition and beseeching God for mercy and help. All of this fits the pattern of a psalm of lamentation. It is the deep cry of the inner person for God—the thirsting of the soul, the longing of the spirit, or hunger of the heart for God. Often this lamentation is an expression more of feeling than of fact; that is, the cry itself is more important than what is stated. This makes the song of lamentation especially suited to instrumental expression, for music usually communicates feelings better than words do.

David's worshipping musicians who ministered before the Lord were also to **give thanks**. David wrote, "I will praise the name of God with a song, and will magnify him with thanksgiving" (Psalm 69:30), and he wanted his musicians to learn to play and sing songs of thanksgiving unto the Lord.

The Psalter has many such psalms; some express individual thanks, and others express collective thanks. Many times when the prophetic song comes forth it will be a melodic expression of thanks both for what God has already done in the past and for what He has promised to do in the future for an individual or for the united Church. Such a song is based upon God's performance or promise, and it will usually be joyful as well as grateful. A good example of this is Psalm 18, in which David spent forty-eight verses telling what God had done for him and then concluded by saying, "Therefore I will give thanks to thee, O LORD, among the heathen, and sing praises unto thy name" (verse 49). When the minds of believers are occupied with thoughts of God's goodness and faithfulness, songs of thanksgiving will burst forth among the people.

The third thing David's musicians were to do was to **praise the Lord**. The Psalms overflow with expressions of praise, and the word "Hallelujah" is generously sprinkled throughout them. On the whole, these praise psalms are more general than the thanksgiving psalms, for the singer's purpose is to magnify the name of God and extol His excellent greatness. So it is among musicians today through whom the prophetic song comes. For those

6

whose spiritual maturity can cause them to see beyond God's beneficent actions to His beautiful Person, songs and music that glorify God in the praise of His being will flow forth like water from a faucet.

We remember...we thank...we praise. And something happens when we do!

### Results of the Prophetic Song

Many glorious things take place when the prophetic song is sung in the Church. There is a **spiritual freedom** brought to those who may be in spiritual bondage. Captives are set free when a prophetic song is sung. The prophetic message is God's instruction; it may be God's written Word expressed musically. As it is sung, those who hear it become aware of the truth, and they are made free. "Awake, awake, Deborah: awake, awake, utter a song: arise, Barak, and lead thy captivity captive..." (Judges 5:12). Anointed music, drenched in the Spirit of God (which is a spiritual song, a song of the Spirit) breaks the power of the enemy and sets the hostages free.

Satan cannot withstand the force of such a word. David played his harp in the presence of the king, and there was such a Divine unction upon his music that the evil spirit troubling Saul was driven away (*see* 1 Samuel 16:23). There is an anointing that breaks yokes (*see* Isaiah 10:27), and it can be demonstrated and released in the prophetic song.

Singing this new song will bring **spiritual victories.** Even in the valley of trouble we can sing the song of the Lord and see victory. Hosea 2:15 declares that Israel will sing in the valley of Achor (Hebrew "trouble") as she did in her younger days, when she came out of Egypt. Those songs were the new songs of Moses and Miriam. God was saying that when Israel would again sing those new songs, as were sung when the deliverance from Egypt

7

was celebrated, God would move victoriously on their behalf. Victory follows the song. The children of Israel saw first-hand, visible demonstrations of this in battle. The "advance forces" were sometimes not the spear-bearers but the music-makers! Psalm 68, which gives us a triumphant picture of God going forth in victory, tells us that "the singers went before, the players on instruments followed after..." (verse 25). In the days of Jehoshaphat, a tremendous victory was won when the king "appointed singers unto the LORD, and that should praise the beauty of holiness, as they went out before the army, and to say, Praise the LORD: for his mercy endureth for ever. And when they began to sing and to praise, the LORD sent ambushments against the children of Ammon, Moab, and mount Seir, which were come against Judah; and they were smitten" (2 Chronicles 20:21,22). The word of the Lord going forth on the wings of melody swept through the enemy forces with the power of the Spirit that anointed that music, and victory came!

The prophetic song leads us into **spiritual fellowship**. It brings us closer to Jesus. There is a sense of His nearness as we hear Him proclaimed and uplifted in the song of the Lord. The same Holy Spirit Who is prompting the prophetic song desires to exalt Jesus, the Lamb of God, and as Christ is lifted up in the song, we are drawn unto Him. Our focus shifts to the One Who is the source and the object of our love. Our expressions of that love come forth from the Spirit within us, and we find that the things of earth do indeed become strangely dim in His beautiful presence. We are no longer concerned with "I, me, and mine" but with "You" and "Yours." We experience a sweet communion with the Lover of our souls. What joy and fulfillment are found in singing that new song as the Spirit gives utterance.

The prophetic song **uplifts** those who are defeated and depressed. When David was "down in the dumps," he would often sing Spirit-inspired songs. Isaiah 61:3 tells us that we can exchange the "spirit of heaviness" for the "garment of praise" (Hebrew *tehilloh*, "praise—laudations of the Spirit"). Often what we wear depicts our state of mind. We need to clothe ourselves with the new songs the Spirit prompts within us; as we do, the old, dirty, tattered garment of depression and mourning is cast off.

Often we find that as we sing the prophetic song, it **testifies** to others of the greatness of our God. "It is a good thing to give thanks unto the LORD, and to sing praises unto thy name, O most High: to shew forth thy lovingkindness...and thy faithfulness..." (Psalm 92:1,2). Spirit-inspired songs proclaim God's nature and character; they speak of all that He is. Multitudes of the Psalms extol God. Undoubtedly David and the other psalmists had no idea, as they sang from their hearts the words that the Spirit inspired, what a witness and blessing those expressions would be for untold generations to come. Yet the testimony remains, and today our hearts also find expression in singing the words that these men sang so long ago.

As the new song with its prophetic touch comes forth, there is often a response of **reverence**. "And he hath put a new song in my mouth, even praise unto our God; many shall see it, and fear, and shall trust in the LORD" (Psalm 40:3). The Hebrew word for "fear" in this verse is *yare*, meaning "reverence, awe, righteous behavior; worship." The emphasis is usually more upon reverence than upon a sense of terror. The prophetic song produces a sense of reverence or awe which may lead to worship as well.

Another result of the prophetic song could be **righteous living**, as we can see from the verse we have just read. If those who hear the prophetic song are unsaved, they may be converted and find that they, too, reverence God. If others are unaccustomed to the expression of the prophetic song, they may experience a persuasion in their hearts that will bring them to a new level of understanding

9

and worship.

Sometimes musicians can move the emotions of a congregation to cry out to God in a confession of sin, an expression of need, or an admission of failure. During a convention in the Washington, D.C. area several years ago, nothing seemed to move the people to respond in worship to God; they even put up strong resistance to the preaching. On the second morning, the speaker felt the Holy Spirit prompting him to go to the organ and play a chorus before the service began. The conference director gave him permission to do this, so he sat down at the organ and began to play the chorus over and over, changing style and going from one key to another, but staying with the melody the Lord had given him. He closed his eyes as he played, and he got so lost in worship that he was totally unaware of anything happening around him.

After awhile he slowly realized that someone was trying to get his attention, so he opened his eyes and looked up. The director motioned to him to stop playing and to look at the platform. Standing at the pulpit was a weeping man, with another next to him, and another next to that one, and so on all the way to the side wall and down the far aisle. When the organ music stopped, the man at the pulpit made a confession of sin and asked forgiveness. After a time of prayer, the next man in line did the same thing, and so did the next, and the next, and the next. It was after 1:00 p.m. before the service dismissed for lunch, and during all that time neither the director nor the speaker had said a word; the anointed music had touched something in those people and caused them to look at themselves and make a fresh commitment to God. What the preaching of the Word had not accomplished, the playing of the Word had done in just one session. That pastor and conference director are now firm believers in "the song of the Lord."

The song of the Lord is far more a musical release of an inner feeling or attitude than it is an expression of a mental concept. While it may teach, this is not its primary purpose. Like the dance, it is best suited for releasing human emotions toward God. Most Christians already know much more than they have responded to or personally entered into, so it could be that the release which the prophetic song brings is more important to their maturity than hearing another sermon would be.

There is clear indication in the Scriptures, from historians, and by scholars of the Hebrew and Greek languages that the prophetic song has its place in the Church. It is not something to be feared. Yet many today are "not sure" about this wonderful manifestation of the Spirit of God. So often we find that we tend to be "down" on something that we're not "up" on. If you have never studied the prophetic song in Scripture, you will have questions about it and may even have problems with it. But, my friend, it is real, it is valid, and it is for us! Just because this seems new to us now does not mean that it originated in the twentieth century. "There is no new thing under the sun" (Ecclesiastes 1:9). In any generation where there has been a revelation of Jesus Christ, there have been songs breathed by the Spirit of God. In past days and again in this day, the prophetic song is being sovereignly experienced among God's people.

# Chapter 2

# Patterns for the Prophetic Song

Praise and worship are not "new things"; the song of the Lord, or the prophetic song, is not a new thing. Believers have been singing to and about the Lord as long as there have been believers, and certainly the voice of the Lord has been heard among His people since the very beginning.

We have already seen how the Psalms abound with examples of songs given by the inspiration of the Spirit. But the Psalms do not have a monopoly on the "songs of the Spirit," for all ten major Bible divisions contain examples. The prophetic song is as fresh as today's move of the Spirit, and yet it is as old as the Word itself.

The **Pentateuch** records the glorious song of Moses which Israel sang after they successfully crossed the Red Sea and watched their enemies drown behind them. This song commemorated the great deliverance God brought them and the greatness of the God Who could bring about such a deliverance. Its theme of redemption is so current that we will sing it in heaven, where it will be joined with the song of the Lamb (*see* Revelation 15:3,4), for both songs are based on the triumph of "It is finished."

In the **historical books** the commissioning of Saul to be Israel's first king was involved with singing prophets (*see* 1 Samuel 10:5,6). Much later, when Nehemiah rebuilt the walls of Jerusalem, he formed two "thanksgiving choirs" to march in opposite directions around the tops of the walls during the dedication ceremony, as a triumphant and joyous expression of thanksgiving unto the Lord for His protection during the construction work and for His Divine help in the construction. What these choirs sang is not recorded; probably the songs were extemporaneous and the words were not so important as the emotion and devotion released by the singing. Some anointed songs fit only a single occasion, while at other times the prophetic song has such a dynamic content that an entire congregation will pick up the song and sing it for months to come. Sometimes the song reaches beyond the local congregation and becomes a message sung widely throughout the Body of Christ. A powerful example of this is the song "All Hail King Jesus," which can lift the singer and the listener into exhilarating realms of worship.

In January of 1977, a prophetic song was born in the heart of a young man named Dave Moody. It was on a Wednesday afternoon as Dave was waiting on the Lord, singing to Jesus at the piano, that the song "All Hail King Jesus" came to his spirit. He said the verse and chorus came very quickly. In about ten minutes, he had the melody line, the chords and the words. Dave said, "When I received the song, it drew me to the Lord. I felt excited, burdened, and stirred, yet I knew I had something from the Lord to give. I sensed quickly it was to be shared. It wasn't for me only. All week, I felt fire in my bones until Sunday, waiting to share this prophetic song. It stirred in my spirit until I shared it at the next service."

That Sunday morning, Dave Moody led the worship and the service began as normal. When the time was appropriate, Dave began to sing the chorus of "All Hail King Jesus" through a few times. However, there seemed to be little response to the song. Dave said "I thought it had flopped. I was closing the song when the assistant Pastor encouraged me to keep it going." Suddenly, like a wave of the Spirit of God, the song impacted all of the worshipping congregation. It seemed that everyone was on their knees declaring Jesus as King.

Eight or nine hundred people were kneeling at their seats and in the aisles with hands lifted. It was the prophetic song that brought this response. People had a revelation of Jesus as King as a result of this song from the Lord.

"All Hail King Jesus" became a favorite in the church and quickly spread through the missionaries from the church to other countries. It spread through the Christian grapevine as worship leaders picked it up and taught it to their churches. It was one of the first songs that exalted Jesus as royalty. Up to that time there were a lot of songs about what Jesus had done for us. This was one of the first that declared who He is. Since then, there have been more anthem type choruses such as "Majesty, I Exalt Thee," "To Thee We Ascribe Glory" and many more. "All Hail King Jesus" was a pivotal song turning our worship to be more God-centered. It was by the impetus of the Holy Spirit through a musician, who was waiting on the Lord that this turn occurred in the body of Christ.

More commonly, however, the song of the moment is a release of the feelings of the moment and does not "stick with" those who hear it. It was sung in the inspiration of the moment, and, like a cut rose, it shared its beauty and fragrance briefly and then faded and died.

The **poetic books**, of course, are filled with songs sung unto and about the Lord. "The song of songs, which is Solomon's" is a good example, for the Song of Solomon is a beautiful series of songs sung by the Bride to the Bridegroom and shared by the

15

Bridegroom with His Bride. From time to time you will hear such antiphonal responses in a congregation during a time of worship. One person sings unto the Lord, and another person prophetically sings God's response to His people. At times the two blend in a beautiful duet, entirely unplanned and unrehearsed but fitting together in a harmony of melody and content that could be directed only by the Spirit of the Lord. The Holy Spirit is a master of music, and when He finds yielded individuals He can blend voices harmoniously with interwoven messages that excite the listeners to praise and worship. Those who have heard congregational singing of the prophetic song both in English and in ecstatic utterances can testify to its musical beauty and to the stirring dynamics of the music and its message.

The **major prophets** contain a great number and variety of examples of what could be called the prophetic song. Isaiah wrote, "Now will I sing to my wellbeloved a song of my beloved touching his vineyard" (Isaiah 5:1), and the song is a parable with a powerful message. The Holy Spirit seems to like to use this format, for we often hear the prophetic song come forth as a simple story sung unto the Lord, or sung as a message from the Lord. As in all parables, the moral truth that is illustrated strikes home to the conscience of the listeners, and when it is given in musical form, it moves the emotions and may produce a result of obedience.

Isaiah also recorded the poem written by Hezekiah after his recovery from his sickness. This hymn of praise and thanksgiving ended with Hezekiah saying, "The LORD was ready to save me: therefore we will sing my songs to the stringed instruments all the days of our life in the house of the LORD" (Isaiah 38:20). Apparently this poem was divided into separate songs which Hezekiah indicated would be sung in the house of the Lord until his dying day (which, thanks to God's mercy, was at least fifteen more years away). Sometimes God gives the song in the privacy of an individual's life, but that song can be sung under the anointing in the congregation of the people and be as fresh and as striking as though it were being composed on the spot. To "sing unto the LORD a new song" (Isaiah 42:10) does not require the giving and the singing of the song to take place simultaneously; it just requires new subject matter, new motivation, and new inspiration. There could easily be a time span of hours or days between the giving of this new song and the singing of it, but it is still a spontaneous song of the Spirit, sung to or about the Lord, that has come as a result of the Spirit's impartation.

In the **minor prophets**, Habakkuk provides an outstanding example of singing a song to the Lord. Chapter one of Habakkuk's book is a dismal complaint about how unfair God was to allow all the things that were happening. But in chapter two God called Habakkuk to a watch-tower experience and showed him that although even more grief and trouble were coming, a Deliverer was also coming. When Habakkuk realized this, he began a prayer inscribed "To the chief singer on my stringed instruments" (3:19), and this prayer was accompanied on a double harp, according to G. Campbell Morgan. The prophet had no song at all until he saw God's Deliverer, and then his song required a double harp for adequate accompaniment. Joyfully he sang, "Although the fig tree shall not blossom, neither shall fruit be in the vines; the labour of the olive shall fail, and the fields shall yield no meat; the flock shall be cut off from the fold, and there shall be no herd in the stalls: yet I will rejoice in the LORD, I will joy in the God of my salvation" (3:17,18). How heaven must have rejoiced to hear this song instead of the complaints of chapter one.

The **Gospels** list several instances of singing, including the time when Christ led His disciples in prayer in the upper room. The parable of the prodigal son speaks of the return of the son being celebrated with music and dancing (*see* Luke 15:25). It is a picture of the rejoicing in the family of God when a wandering son returns to the Father. Who could deny that this would be a song of the Lord—a song of the Lord's rejoicing. Isn't it fitting for the Holy Spirit to break forth into song when a sinning son repents and returns home? Sometimes it is even the son who breaks forth into joyful singing, and sometimes it is a member of the family who shares in God's great rejoicing.

In the one historical book in the New Testament—the **book of Acts**—we find the account of the time Paul and Silas were illegally arrested and beaten and placed in stocks in the inner dungeon. Bodies aching with pain, and minds confused with these unexpected happenings, "at midnight Paul and Silas prayed, and sang praises unto God: and the prisoners heard them" (Acts 16:25). From the depths of their spirits they were pouring out praises and expressing their confidence in God. It was a song to the Lord, it was a song about the Lord, and it certainly was a song inspired by the Lord, not by their circumstances. It so reached God that He intervened with an earthquake and the conversion of the jailer. Certainly that was a song that produced a response.

As we've already mentioned frequently, in the **Pauline epistles** Paul often spoke of "spiritual songs," declaring that being filled with the Spirit and with the Word would bring an overflow of melodious praises unto God (*see* Ephesians 5:19; Colossians 3:16). We can't emphasize too much that someone who wants to be a channel for singing the prophetic song needs to stay full of the Word and the Spirit, for the Word is the theme of that song, and the Holy Spirit is its inspiration. God, not the Christian music industry, is the inspiration for our song! Since "of the abundance of the heart his mouth speaketh" (Luke 6:45), the musician needs to keep his heart filled with God and His Word, or else, as we've heard too often, the song will be a dirge of fear, failure, and frustration.

Portions of Paul's writings can be considered prophetic songs; for example, Romans 11:33-36, which begins with the words "O the depth of the riches both of the wisdom and knowledge of God!" and concludes with "For of him, and through him, and to him, are all things: to whom be glory for ever. Amen." Ephesians 5:14 is regarded as the most convincing evidence of hymnology in the early Church: "Awake thou that sleepest, and arise from the dead, and Christ shall give thee light." In writing to Timothy, Paul made the declaration "Now unto the King eternal, immortal, invisible, the only wise God, be honour and glory for ever and ever. Amen" (1 Timothy 1:17). Ralph Martin points out that the phrase "King eternal" is very similar to the expression "King of the ages," which "is exactly the phrase used at Jewish table-prayers ('Blessed be Thou, O Lord our God, King of the ages') and in synagogue praise."[1] Another song in Paul's writings to Timothy which may be considered prophetic is 1 Timothy 3:16: "God was manifest in the flesh, justified in the Spirit, seen of angels, preached unto the Gentiles, believed on in the world, received up into glory." This is a good example of the difference between a hymn and a chorus such as we would sing today; rather than being a simple declaration of honor and praise to God, this song makes a doctrinal statement.

Philippians 2:6-11 and Colossians 1:15-20 are also examples of songs in Paul's writings. The song in Philippians possibly had six stanzas. Of the song in Colossians, Ralph Martin says that "three pairs of lines are precisely correspondent in the two parts of the hymn. The vocabulary also is unusual and the whole 'betrays the hand of an exacting composer' who penned this noble tribute to exhibit the primacy of Christ in the twin realms of Creation and Redemption."[2]

Even the **general epistles** make provision for the prophetic song in saying, "If any man speak, let him speak as the oracles of God;

if any man minister, let him do it as of the ability which God giveth: that God in all things may be glorified through Jesus Christ, to whom be praise and dominion for ever and ever. Amen" (1 Peter 4:11). While this does not directly speak of singing, it does speak of ministry, and Peter had just instructed, "As every man hath received the gift, even so minister the same one to another, as good stewards of the manifold grace of God" (1 Peter 4:10). Music is both a gift and a ministry, and if this gift is received from the Lord it must be shared with the Church of the Lord Jesus Christ. Jesus spoke a parable about gifts, or "talents" that were not properly used and so were taken away and given to one who would correctly utilize them (*see* Matthew 25:14-29). A song that the Spirit births within us needs to be shared so that the entire Body of Christ can be edified.

The tenth, and final, major division of the Bible is the book of prophecy in the New Testament: the **Revelation** of Jesus Christ. Not only is the song of Moses coupled with the song of the Lamb to be sung by the saints in heaven, as we have already seen (*see* Revelation 15:3,4), but the four living creatures with the elders sang "a new song, saying, Thou art worthy to take the book, and to open the seals thereof: for thou wast slain, and hast redeemed us to God by thy blood out of every kindred, and tongue, and people, and nation; and hast made us unto our God kings and priests: and we shall reign on the earth" (Revelation 5:9,10). Later a vast multitude sang "as it were a new song before the throne" (14:3). How could one be in the direct presence of the God of glory and not sing this song!

So we can see that the foundation has been laid throughout the pages of Scripture for the manifestation of the Spirit of God in the prophetic song. Surely God is a singing God!

## The Singing Deity

We have spoken of singing **about** the Lord—extolling His name, nature, and acts—and singing **to** the Lord—expressing to Him what is in our hearts and spirits. But we must also remember that there is singing **of** the Lord. We have clearly seen that the Spirit is a singing Spirit—so obviously the other members of the Godhead also sing.

It is totally foreign and actually amazing to us to entertain the thought that God sings. But why should it be? When we acknowledge God as the Creator Who made all things, it is neither preposterous nor unreasonable to think that He sings. If He can create music, surely He can sing. God is not limited in His ability. What a joy it is for the singing musician to realize that the Chief Musician Himself sings. The Bible is clear on this, for both the Old and New Testaments tell us that God does indeed sing and that in fact, He rejoices in singing. The prophet Zephaniah declared, "The LORD thy God in the midst of thee is mighty; he will save, he will rejoice over thee with joy; he will rest in his love, he will joy over thee with singing" (Zephaniah 3:17), while Hebrews speaks of Jesus saying, "I will declare thy name unto my brethren, in the midst of the church will I sing praise unto thee" (Hebrews 2:12).

I have often wondered what would inspire such joy that the Lord would sing. The apostle John gave us a glimpse of the heart of God when he wrote, "I have no greater joy than to hear that my children walk in truth" (3 John 4). Surely if the heart of an earthly "father in the faith" had such feelings, how much more must the heart of the heavenly Father rejoice over His obedient, loving children!

God is revealing mysteries and principles to perfect the Church. Several years ago very little was understood about musical praise and worship, though there are thousands of Scriptures on the

21

subject—well over eight hundred on music alone! In those days we remained steeped in tradition rather than acting on biblical truth. Our traditions brought stability and anchored our faith, but they also anchored us to "the way we've always done it." But now God is moving in fresh ways. Isaiah proclaimed God's words: "Behold, I will do a new thing; now it shall spring forth; shall ye not know it? I will even make a way in the wilderness, and rivers in the desert. This people have I formed for myself; they shall shew forth my praise" (Isaiah 43:19,21).

These Scriptures held no revelation for us a decade ago. But now we have such revelation that we no longer must remain in the darkness of the past but can walk in the illumination of His Word. We have truth available to us, and we are also responsible to embrace that revealed truth and to walk in it.

As God quickens this truth—makes it alive to you and in you—and you understand that the Lord not only sings but desires to sing through you, your praise and worship will change. You will begin to hear the sound of the Lord as He moves in the midst of the congregation. You will cry, "Lord, sing through me!" When He answers that prayer, you will recognize His voice...and it will sound incredibly like yours. You will listen during intimate times of worship and will hear Him singing. But He sounds so much like you and those around you! Is that really Jesus singing?

We have just seen from Hebrews that Jesus sings praise in the midst of His Church. It's interesting to note that He sings not in the concert hall or at the television station (though that is possible, of course) but in His Church. Singing is scripturally connected with His house or His people gathering together, and His voice is associated with praise. Biblical praise may not be a part of the concert hall or the television station, but it must always be a part of His Church.

Moses, the mighty servant of God, testified that "the LORD

is my strength and song'' (Exodus 15:2). Moses loved to sing, and God was his song! Exodus 15 gives us that wonderful victory song which Moses and the people sang after their miraculous deliverance from the Egyptians. It was a fresh expression of joy and renewed faith in God, perhaps accompanied by musical instruments; in fact, verse 20 says that Miriam and the women not only sang and danced but played the timbrels. On another occasion Moses ''spake in the ears of all the congregation of Israel the words of this song, until they were ended'' (Deuteronomy 31:30)—a song which occupies the next forty-three verses. God had given Moses this song and had also instructed him to teach it to the children of Israel, for ''the LORD said unto Moses...Now therefore write ye this song for you, and teach it the children of Israel: put it in their mouths, that this song may be a witness for me against the children of Israel...it shall not be forgotten out of the mouths of their seed....Moses therefore wrote this song the same day, and taught it the children of Israel'' (Deuteronomy 31:16,19,21,22). Perhaps God even rehearsed the song in Moses' ear. When Moses sang, the people heard God's song. They heard the prophetic song of the Lord, for when Moses sang, the Spirit of God was singing through him. Moses received a word from God, and instead of delivering it as a spoken prophetic utterance, he sang it according to the commandment of God.

Yes, the Godhead sings. Some men of God believe that at creation the world was *sung* rather than *spoken* into existence, that there was singing when the foundation of the world was laid, for when God revealed His omnipotence to Job, He asked, ''Where wast thou when I laid the foundations of the earth?...Whereupon are the foundations thereof fastened? or who laid the cornerstone thereof; when the morning stars sang together, and all the sons of God shouted for joy?'' (Job 38:4,6,7). Jesus declared, ''I am...the bright and morning star'' (Revelation 22:16). What a celestial sound must have echoed through the heavens when this song was sung amid shouts of joy from the mighty sons of God!

"Rejoicing and gladness" are the themes of the song that the Lord sings among His people. The Spirit of God not only sings praise to the Father in the congregation; He inspires songs that express the Father's great joy in His children. God is happy with His redeemed ones, and He bursts forth with songs that bring wellsprings of joy in their hearts. A true manifestation of the song of the Lord will be joy in the hearts of singer and listener alike. God does not sing His judgments; He sings His joy! How well David expressed this: "Shout joyfully to the LORD, all the earth; break forth in song, rejoice, and sing praises. Sing to the LORD with the harp, with the harp and the sound of a psalm, with trumpets and the sound of a horn; shout joyfully before the LORD, the King" (Psalm 98:4-6, NKJV).

David also declared, "Thou shalt compass me about with songs of deliverance" (Psalm 32:7). The Lord will surround us with songs of victorious deliverance. His songs are not dirges of despair but songs of might, victory, and faith!

Every Christian should experience God singing through him, and every musician must know God in his music. It is far more than writing a song and asking the Lord to anoint *your* song; it is letting God sing *His* song through you. It is bringing forth songs of the Holy Spirit—those "new songs" of which the psalmist spoke when he wrote, "And he hath put a new song in my mouth, even praise unto our God" (Psalm 40:3). "Sing unto the Lord," indeed, but come to know the Lord unto Whom you sing, and learn how that Lord sings to and through His people.

## Singing in the Early Church

There is a sense in Scripture, which seems to be confirmed by history, that the early Church experienced the same presence of

Christ in their midst as we do today, and that the manifestations of the Holy Spirit were present then even as they are now. This would include the prophetic song. There is little doubt that the founding fathers of the New Testament Church experienced the singing of spontaneous Spirit-given melodies in their worship, or that the prophetic voice was heard in their gatherings on a regular basis. It is also believed by many that musical instruments were used in their worship.

Paul testified that he worshipped the God of his fathers and believed everything written in the Law and the prophets (*see* Acts 24:14). When Paul established churches and set the worship order, he did so according to the scriptural pattern of that time.

The early Church began its existence within the framework of the Jewish faith. On the surface it would appear that this group of disciples was a party within the Jewish fold. But what marked them as different was that they believed the Messiah had come. T. W. Manson states, "The first disciples were Jews by birth and upbringing, and it is a priori probable that they would bring into the new community some, at least, of the religious usages to which they had long been accustomed,"[3] while Ralph Martin observes that "the background of early Christian worship must be sought in these two Jewish institutions of the Temple and the synagogue."[4]

We know that the singing of Scripture, probably in the form of a chant or Hebrew cantillation, occurred in both the Temple and the synagogues. Christianity entered into an inheritance of an already-established pattern of worship in both the Temple ritual and the synagogue liturgy.

Hymn-singing was developed in the first century B.C. by the sect of the Therapeutae. Philo described a typical meeting in which one of the group "stands up and sings a hymn to God, either a new one which he has himself composed, or an old one by an earlier composer. The others follow one by one in fitting order, while all listen in complete silence, except when they have to sing the refrains and responses." In the evening gatherings the men and women were separated at first; in their separate groups they would sing hymns, sometimes antiphonally, often accompanying the anthems with rhythmical movements. "Then 'divinely inspired, the men and women together, having become one choir' sing 'hymns of thanks to the Savior God.' "[5]

The singing of Divine praises may not have been well developed in the Palestinian synagogues of the first century. No doubt the exiled Jews of the Dispersion were more advanced in the singing of psalms and praises than were their more conservative countrymen in Palestine. But nonetheless, those early believers had a desire to express their thanksgiving and praise to God in musical form.

There was a distinct difference between the traditional hymns everyone knew and sang in the early Church and the prophetic songs which were new and spontaneous. Paul admonished the believers, "...when ye come together, every one of you hath a psalm..." (1 Corinthians 14:26). Paul also testified, "I will sing with the spirit, and I will sing with the understanding also" (1 Corinthians 14:15). We have already noted that on more than one occasion Paul spoke of "spiritual songs"—more specifically, songs inspired by the Spirit. In *Worship in the Early Church*, Ralph Martin says, "It is not likely, therefore, that Paul would speak of 'psalms inspired by the Spirit...' if he intended the reference to be to the borrowing of traditional odes from the hymn-book of the Jewish Psalter. Compositions which were spontaneously 'inspired' and created for the occasion are much more probably in view."[6]

The first Christians, then, sang psalms, hymns, and spiritual songs. Since the early Church was born out of the structure of synagogue worship, and since the Talmud declares that man must utter first praise and then prayer, no doubt those believers would

26

open their gatherings with corporate praise. The singing of psalms headed the list of "things to do when coming together" (1 Corinthians 14:26), so that was probably the first order of service. The word used in that passage for psalm is *psalmos*, which means a set piece of music with accompaniment by a musical instrument. In general, the term "psalms" refers to Christian odes, perhaps patterned after the Old Testament psalter. "Hymns" would be longer compositions with a continuing theme, perhaps doctrinal. Such hymns can be found in the writing of the New Testament itself. "Spiritual songs" are "snatches of spontaneous praise which the inspiring Spirit placed on the lips of the enraptured worshipper, as 1 Corinthians 14:15 implies."[7] Apparently, Spirit-breathed songs were not uncommon in the worship of the first-century believers.

## The Prophetic Song in Today's Church

But this was not just for those believers back then; I believe the song of the Lord is a part of our present-day worship. It is present truth—a part of the Tabernacle of David that God declared He would rebuild in the last days. The prophet Amos recorded what was to come: "In that day will I raise up the tabernacle of David, the fallen hut or booth and close up its breaches, and I will raise up its ruins, and I will build it as in the days of old" (Amos 9:11, Amplified Bible). David had prepared a place for the Ark (*see* 1 Chronicles 15:1), and God is again seeking a place where His presence may dwell. As I travel and preach in churches across the country, I am amazed at the number of pastors who believe that God has revealed the truth of David's Tabernacle to them alone. What a joy it is for them to discover that other churches worship as they do! What confirmation that the Father is seeking worshippers!

It is our responsibility to embrace truth, and, more importantly, to walk in truth. We must not only understand the present truth of worship but must also be personally involved in it. The Scriptures tell us to "be established in present truth...ye shall know the truth, and the truth shall make you free" (2 Peter 1:12; John 8:32). We need freedom from man's non-biblical traditions and the unscriptural trappings of religion. God wants us to be free to soar in worship as an eagle in the heavens.

The apostle Paul made a strong commitment to truth when he wrote, "...after the way which they call heresy, so worship I the God of my fathers, believing all things which are written in the law and in the prophets" (Acts 24:14). Paul unequivocally put himself on the side of truth. He believed what was written in the books of Moses. He believed what the prophets had proclaimed. Others, too, embraced the Word of God. James quoted the words of the prophet about the restoration of David's tabernacle (*see* Acts 15:16), and Peter pronounced that "ye are a chosen generation, a royal priesthood, an holy nation, a peculiar people; that ye should shew forth the praises of him who hath called you out of darkness into his marvellous light" (1 Peter 2:9). This is a generation to whom praise and worship is being restored, even as the psalmist foresaw so many years ago: "This shall be written for the generation to come: and the people which shall be created shall praise the LORD" (Psalm 102:18). No wonder David could joyfully sing, "And he hath put a new song in my mouth, even praise unto our God..." (Psalm 40:3).

The presence of the prophetic song is a manifestation of the Spirit (*see* Colossians 3:16). As we more clearly understand the nature of prophecy and its various expressions, we will be better able to hear what the Spirit would say to us and sing what the Spirit would say through us.

# Chapter 3
# The Role of Prophecy

If we are going to understand the prophetic song and, more importantly, become personally involved with it, we must first have a clear comprehension of prophecy. We must understand what it is, what its purpose is, and how it is expressed. We see, of course, that the two elements which make up the prophetic song are the musical aspect and the prophetic aspect. Obviously the prophetic element is the more important because it is the Divine ingredient, and the music is the realm through which that Divine factor is expressed. The expression would still be Divine whether it was sung or spoken, but the music without the Divine element would just be music.

Often we think of prophecy mainly in the sense of being predictive, that is, telling something to happen in the future, but this is only one aspect of prophecy. Prophets do foretell future events, but prophecy is both foretelling and forthtelling.

Prophecy is God speaking to His people through a person. To prophesy is to speak (or sing), by inspiration of the Holy Spirit, a prediction or a discourse of exhortation, edification, or comfort. We know that prophecy is listed as one of the gifts of the Holy

Spirit—one of what we generally call "the nine gifts of the Spirit" (*see* 1 Corinthians 12), one of the three "vocal" gifts. Paul spoke at length about prophecy in 1 Corinthians 14, and admonished believers to "desire...that ye may prophesy. Wherefore, brethren, covet to prophesy..." (verses 1,39). He was speaking of prophecy in general terms, but prophecy encompasses more than one realm.

There are four dimensions of prophecy: prophecy of Scripture, the office of the prophet, the gift of prophecy, and the spirit of prophecy. Let us look at these individually.

**Prophecy of Scripture**

All biblical revelation spoken by the prophets is prophecy of Scripture. We know that "all scripture is given by inspiration of God, and is profitable for doctrine, for reproof, for correction, for instruction in righteousness" (2 Timothy 3:16). That which we call "the Bible" is also called "the canon of Scripture" because it has been established and accepted as the divinely inspired Word of God. There is no higher revelation than this, nor is there a higher realm of prophetic expression.

The term "given by inspiration of God" literally means "God breathed." So, the Scripture can be considered prophetic in nature in the sense that God spoke it, and therefore when it is sung, it carries that prophetic sense with it. What God has spoken, He has spoken; He neither adds to it nor takes away from it. Peter reminded us that "knowing this first...no prophecy of the scripture is of any private interpretation. For the prophecy came not in old time by the will of man; but holy men of God spake as they were moved by the Holy Ghost" (2 Peter 1:20,21). God's Word is the final voice and authority. No expression or revelation will be higher, for, as Solomon observed, "There is no new thing under the sun. Is there any thing whereof it may be said, See, this is new? it hath been already of old time, which was before us"

(Ecclesiastes 1:9,10). There is no "new" revelation—only revelation that is new to us. God is not adding to His Word but is revealing it to us—adding to our knowledge, enlightening our spiritual understanding, showing us hidden truths and deeper meanings that we have not understood before. Whatever is spoken forth as prophecy must meet the standard of the greatest prophetic expression of all: the Word of God. True prophecy will originate with or can be confirmed by the Scriptures. Prophecy of Scripture is not present in the Church today. The Canon of Scripture is complete and the Father teaches us in His Word we are not to add to the prophecies of the Bible.

## The Prophetic Office

One who holds the office of a prophet is endowed with the ability to prophesy at any time. This is a greater or higher dimension than the gift or spirit of prophecy, for it embodies a life style as well as a message. The person in this office is not a prophet because he speaks prophetic messages; he speaks those prophetic messages because he is a prophet.

The prophetic call and anointing come by God's choice and only by God's choice. Man cannot achieve this office by his own desire or efforts. God told Jeremiah, "Before I formed thee in the belly I knew thee; and before thou camest forth out of the womb I sanctified thee, and I ordained thee a prophet unto the nations" (Jeremiah 1:5). God selects whom He wills, to speak what He wills, when He wills. He doesn't ask man's opinion.

The prophetic office is one of the ascension gift ministries given to the New Testament Church (*see* Ephesians 4:11). The prophet may, of course, minister edification, exhortation, and comfort, but he may also operate in the spheres of guidance, rebuke, judgment, correction, prediction, or revelation. No one should presume to minister in this realm unless he has been commissioned

31

by the Lord to the office of a prophet, so of course no one who sings the prophetic song should attempt to so minister unless he knows that he has been placed in that prophetic office.

In the Old Testament, prophets were called "oracles," which Webster defines as "a person through whom a deity is believed to speak." This word is found in the New Testament in Peter's admonition "If any man speak, let him speak as the oracles of God" (1 Peter 4:11). Prophetic messages were also called oracles, for Paul wrote that "unto them [the Jews] were committed the oracles of God" (Romans 3:2).

Those who do manifest the prophetic office proclaim God's presence, purpose, and message, whether in word or in song. "Surely the Lord GOD will do nothing but he revealeth his secret unto his servants the prophets" (Amos 3:7).

There is a great responsibility involved for one who carries this prophetic anointing. If his prophecies are to be profitable, he must be "prophet-able"; his life must demonstrate the message even as his words declare it, and he must function in uprightness of heart, correctness of attitude and motivation, and obedience to the One from Whom the message comes. Speaking or singing, he must do so as God's mouthpiece. More than once we are told in the Old Testament that "the LORD spake by his servants the prophets, saying..." (*see* 2 Kings 21:10, 24:2). Man did the vocalizing, but the words were God's. "...the Lord GOD hath spoken, who can but prophesy?" (Amos 3:8).

### The Prophetic Gift

The gift of prophecy is a gift of the Holy Spirit that finds residence in some believers as a ministry to the Body of Christ. Not every believer has this gift, though he has been filled with the Holy Spirit, for it is up to the Spirit to distribute it "severally as he will" (*see* 1 Corinthians 12:11). Those who have this gift may prophesy regularly, for the gift is resident within them; there is no need to wait for the spirit of prophecy.

This gift is to be used for edification, exhortation, and comfort (*see* 1 Corinthians 14:3). Prophetic **edification** is the building up of a believer in his spiritual life. Words of edification strengthen believers in their faith, in their walk, and in their relationship with God. Prophetic **exhortation** is a stirring up of the believers. It applies truth to behavior and serves to keep believers from straying from God. It provides motivation, encouragement, and challenge in Christian living, and sometimes brings words of admonition or warning. Prophetic **comfort** is the consolation, the cheering, the assurance, and the revealed nearness of the Holy Spirit to those in difficult situations.

There should be no judgment, rebuke, or correction in the prophecy that comes forth from one exercising the prophetic gift. Let those who have this gift sing their prophecies if they so choose—but only that which will result in the building up, the stirring up, and the cheering up of the saints of God.

### The Spirit of Prophecy

The spirit of prophecy is the quickening (or anointing) of the Holy Spirit, in which all may prophesy. When this unction is present, anyone may enter into the prophetic flow; "ye may all prophesy one by one, that all may learn, and all may be comforted" (1 Corinthians 14:31). The spirit of prophecy is the Holy Spirit's mantle of prophetic anointing given from time to time to a believer (or believers), resulting in the speaking forth of the word of the Lord.

The key to understanding this realm is that it happens from time to time. Without this special endowment, an individual who does not hold the office of a prophet or have the gift of prophecy could not prophesy the word of the Lord. (He could respond to a situation

33

with an appropriate word, but unless the spirit of prophecy is present, it is not the word of the Lord, and he dare not attach God's name to it.) He is enabled to prophesy by the presence of the cloud of God's prophetic anointing.

Someone who prophesies only occasionally is giving evidence that he has neither the office nor the gift of prophecy but functions only when the spirit of prophecy is present. "Paul, in 1 Corinthians 14:24,31, states that all may prophesy. Yet Paul clearly separates this from the office of a prophet and by contextual implication [from] the gift of prophecy by the phrasing of his question in 1 Corinthians 12:29, 'All are not prophets, are they?' requiring a negative answer in the Greek form."[1]

At times the prophetic cloud may be over an entire congregation, and anyone could flow in prophecy at that point if he exercised faith to do so. This is what happened when the seventy elders who assisted Moses in leading Israel all prophesied as the spirit of prophecy came upon them (Numbers 11:24-30). Saul experienced a similar anointing when he met a company of prophets and prophesied among them. He himself was not a prophet, and did not have the gift of prophecy, and yet he did speak the word of the Lord under a prophetic anointing.

Most prophetic songs fit into the realm of the spirit of prophecy, for, relatively speaking, there are more "ordinary believers" than there are genuine prophets or even persons possessing the gift of prophecy. It stands to reason that far more people will prophesy by entering into this flow than by exercising either the office or the gift of prophecy. Yet there is no reason why someone with the office of a prophet or the gift of prophecy could not sing when prophesying.

It is also possible (and worth considering) that the prophetic song is a melodic expression of a "word of wisdom" or a "word of knowledge" (both listed with prophecy in the "nine gifts of the

Spirit" in 1 Corinthians 12). Even the gift of faith could be expressed in song, as when Moses was commanded to have the elders sing during a water shortage: "...the LORD spake unto Moses, Gather the people together, and I will give them water. Then Israel sang this song, Spring up, O well; sing ye unto it" (Numbers 21:16,17). The water came in response to the song! But no matter what "gift" is manifested, it is still an operation of the Spirit of God, and it is God's communication to His people.

A practical example of this involves one of the very first times that I remember receiving the prophetic song—shortly after I was birthed in the Truth and experience of worship. It was a Sunday morning service at Glad Tidings Christian Fellowship in Vancouver, B.C. The worship leader was leading from the organ as often he did on Sunday mornings. A worship team of singers was present on the platform adding beautiful harmonies to the melodies of the congregation's praise. There was a time in the service when the songs stopped and spontaneous praise began to fill that 900-seat auditorium. The electricity of God's presence charged the atmosphere as people were singing songs straight from their hearts to God. Jesus had so raptured their spirits they were composing melodies and lyrics all at the same time, right on the spot.

In the midst of these songs a strange thing happened to me; I sensed a burden deep in my spirit and a sudden nervousness came upon me. It was not until a few minutes later that I realized what was happening. The burden of the prophetic was arising from within me and my flesh was already nervous with the possibility that I would be publically prophesying. The deep awareness of the Holy Spirit's unction from within and sudden prophetic inspiration both came to my spirit at one time.

The words came first so I thought this is to be a spoken prophecy.

I've heard a cry throughout the land
People just cannot understand
The Word of the Lord
And the ways of your God
So I'm raising up sons
And I'm raising up daughters, in Zion.

Only the first six lines seemed to come and I didn't know how
it would end. But I was willing to step out in faith and speak what
God had given me. I watched for openings in the service to speak
but the worship was so intense. The people went on singing in
the Spirit for about 15 minutes. When the praise decrescendoed
enough for me to speak the word God had given me another
prophecy came from a man across the sanctuary. I anxiously waited
for him to finish because what the Holy Spirit was saying through
him seemed very similar to what God had given me. However
as soon as he ended a woman toward the back began to prophesy.
The nervousness inside me grew, my heart began beating faster.
Did God really want me to prophesy? Then why didn't He allow
me opportunity to speak? Tension in my throat and stomach
mounted. I knew what I sensed was God, and yet I wasn't sure.
Some people had told me when God wanted them to prophesy their
right hand would get warm. Others had said they would receive
other kinds of signs. I didn't have a sign—just a "gut" feeling.
No one had told me how to prophesy or what to expect. While
I was waiting I rolled the prophetic word over in my spirit, and
more came to me.

I, the Lord, am moving on the young
I've said they shall be strong
In the Words of the Lord
In the ways of their God

Them will I teach
To do my will, in Zion.

My Spirit shall be upon my people
They shall go forth in my Name.
With the Word of the Lord
And the truth of their God
Feeding hungry souls
The bread of life, that's in Zion.

As the service continued several more prophecies came but as soon as they ended, the congregation burst into praise. When all this finally finished the service moved into the preaching of the Word and then ended. I never gave the prophetic word God had given me.

In the car about half way home that afternoon the words of the prophecy came up in my spirit again and there seemed to be a fresh anointing. The excitement returned as I was caught up in the prophecy again. All of the sudden I began to sing it in my head. The words seemed to be carried freely out of my spirit on the wings of a melody.

When we walked into the house I quickly picked up my guitar and sang it over and over. I turned on a tape recorder so I wouldn't forget it. I was elated, my first prophetic song was birthed. The song was entitled "Sons and Daughters" and was recorded on my first solo album in 1978. I sang it in services across the country and the prophetic mantle remained on the song because often I would prophesy when the song concluded.

What an experience! What a release! I had tasted something that caused my spirit to hunger for more. I wanted to sing the prophetic song again.

**Words Used in Scripture**

There are several different words in the Old Testament that are used for prophecy or prophesying. Some emphasize the experience of receiving the prophetic message from God; some deal with the experience of transmitting the prophetic message to others.

One Hebrew word used often is *roeh [rooh]*, "to see." Its root means "to look at" or "to behold" and is used in relation to the prophet "seeing" God's message—that is, perceiving what God wants to say. A second, related word is *chozeh [khozoh]*, which means "to perceive, see in a vision, prophesy." Like *roeh*, it deals with the receiving of the Divine message. "Thou hast heard, see all this; and will ye not declare it?" (Isaiah 48:6). We find in Isaiah 13:1 and Habakkuk 1:1 that the prophets "saw" the burden (Hebrew *massa*, indicative of a prophetic song) given by God.

This word *massa* speaks of a burden or weight, like a heavy load which is carried. God's message is a burden to the messenger, for he has been chosen to communicate a Divine imperative, and no matter how accurately he may have heard God's voice, he feels the heavy responsibility of causing others to understand what God said. *Massa* can also mean the lifting up of the soul; when someone receives a prophetic song, it may seem that his soul is rising, for it soars in ecstasy as it sings God's word. This is the definition often associated with the Temple musicians such as Chenaniah, the master, who brought forth musical prophecy (*see* 1 Chronicles 15:22).

*Massa* also suggests a restoration, for one goal of prophecy is to build up the hearers. Although God's message may be heavy or severe, it is intended for guidance, so it is still an "uplifting" prophecy. Prophecy is positive even when it deals with negative issues.

A message received from God is not prophecy until it is communicated. There are two elements present in the communication of God's word: the human activity of the person, and the Divine activity of God. The prophetic message is both the words of God and the words of the prophet. God is speaking, and yet man's voice is heard. Man cannot speak without God, and God chooses to speak through man. It is the same with the prophetic song. Some say it is only a musician "jamming" or a singer "improvising," but it is really God singing, for He is prompting the song.

The **Divine** element is contained in the Hebrew word *nataf [notaph]*, which means "to drop"—to fall as drops of rain. Words of prophecy are pictured as raindrops, falling from heaven. The prophetic song is a shower from heaven coming like rain upon the earth.

The **human** element is seen as water flowing from the lips of the one who prophesies. The Hebrew word is *naba*, meaning "to flow, boil up or over; to bubble or pour forth (abundantly); to gush" (*see* Exodus 7:1,2; Proverbs 15:28). Sometimes the prophetic message arises as a mighty torrent from within and then spills forth. Speaking of the Spirit, Jesus declared, "He that believeth on me, as the scripture hath said, out of his belly ['heart,' NKJV] shall flow rivers of living water" (John 7:38). If the Spirit will come forth from the heart of man—and "out of the abundance of the heart the mouth speaketh" (Matthew 12:34)—then surely the words of the Spirit will come pouring forth like a cascading river after a rainstorm.

There is another Hebrew word which is transliterated *naba* and means "to speak/sing by inspiration." This word is used many, many times throughout the Old Testament where we find the words "prophesy" or "prophesied." It, too, speaks of a man's activity. In the New Testament we find the Greek word *propheteuo*, which means "to foretell events; to speak under inspiration; to exercise the prophetic office."

A key feature of prophecy is that it is a revelation directly from God to a person. Both the Divine and human elements must be present. A false prophecy would be something that comes from a person's own imagination, perhaps as a reaction to a situation or an emotion, but without a Divine agency at work. Concerning false prophets, God said, "I have not sent these prophets, yet they ran: I have not spoken to them, yet they prophesied" (Jeremiah 23:21). The calling of a prophet is to wait until God has spoken before giving a message. If he does not hear God speak, he dares not speak for God.

## Judging Prophecy and the Prophetic Song

The Word declares that all prophecy should be judged (*see* 1 Corinthians 14:29), so therefore the prophetic song should also be judged. Prophecy always has the potential of mixture because the human is present along with the Divine; the channel through which the prophecy comes is fallible. The God-inspired word (or prophetic song) could be mixed with the speaker's (or singer's) imagination and come out tainted. There may be a correct reception from God of the word, but the individual could incorrectly or imperfectly communicate it.

The prophetic song, as any prophetic expression, can be tested in six ways. First, the prophetic word should be tested by **the written Word**. As we said earlier, true prophecy originates with or can be confirmed by the Scriptures. Sometimes a prophecy will be unscriptural in content. Paul told us to reject the bad content and retain the good. "Despise not prophesyings. Prove all things; hold fast that which is good" (1 Thessalonians 5:20,21). Does the prophetic song conform in content to the principles and precepts of God's written Word? Does it speak according to the whole of Scripture? Is it in line with specific exhortations in the Bible?

The second test is the **character** of the prophetic song. What is the spirit in which the prophetic song is given? Does it condemn? Remember that the Holy Spirit never speaks in condemnation—in conviction, yes, but not in condemnation. There may be genuine rebuke or correction (given through one who has the office of a prophet), but it will be given in a spirit of tenderness and with the purpose of restoration. A prophetic utterance given in a harsh tone or spirit that would leave the hearer devastated and condemned is not of God.

The third test of prophecy is its **fulfillment**—especially predictive prophetic songs. If the prophecy is fulfilled, that is the proof that its content was divinely inspired and accurate. "When a prophet speaketh in the name of the LORD, if the thing follow not, nor come to pass, that is the thing which the LORD hath not spoken, but the prophet hath spoken it presumptuously" (Deuteronomy 18:22). Obviously, then, if the thing comes to pass, it was the thing which the Lord spoke.

The fourth test is the **conduct** of the individual's life. Scripture requires us to suspect the prophecy if the life style of the one prophesying is not righteous. "For from the prophets of Jerusalem is profaneness gone forth into all the land. Thus said the LORD of hosts, Hearken not unto the words of the prophets that prophesy unto you: they make you vain: they speak a vision of their own heart, and not out of the mouth of the LORD" (Jeremiah 23:15, 16). It is important to try the spirits of the singers of the prophetic song. "Beloved, believe not every spirit, but try the spirits whether they are of God: because many false prophets are gone out into the world" (1 John 4:1). There must be not only proven ministry but proven lives to substantiate that ministry.

The fifth test is the **confirmation of the Spirit**. A prophetic song can be tested by whether or not it bears witness with our inner man through the Holy Spirit Who dwells in us. Romans 8:16 says that "the Spirit itself beareth witness with our spirit." We do need to be aware that this is the least reliable method of judging prophecy or the prophetic song because our own spirits can be misled. "Caution should be exercised against indiscriminate accepting or rejecting of prophetic words on this basis alone. This means of proving a prophetic word should be coupled with one of the other ways of testing a word. Local church leadership must make the final judgment call on these matters."[2]

The sixth test is the **confirmation of other witnesses**. This is especially important when the prophetic word involves significant decisions or changes in direction. Again, this relates to the function of the office of a prophet. There is a need for at least one other witness to such a word. Perhaps it is a confirmation of a previous prophecy. By two or three witnesses every word shall be established (*see* 2 Corinthians 13:1). It is important to understand that the judging of such prophecy should be left to the spiritual leadership in the church because they should be more sensitive to and aware of spiritual matters in the lives of the people for whom they have been given oversight. They are the ones who pray for their people and must give account to God of their leadership. If they are true shepherds, their hearts are concerned with God's best for the people.

While it is true that prophecy is to be judged, and indeed must be judged, it would be wrong to become so judgmental of the prophecy that its message is missed. Those who hear prophecy have a responsibility to respond to it. True prophecy should be received with faith and with a confident expectation that God has done and will do all that He has said in the prophetic utterance. The fact that the prophecy is sung instead of spoken does not change this. What is heard should be mixed with faith (the substance of things hoped for and the evidence of things not seen) so that the song will bring the results that God desired and planned when He gave the song. It may be that the music will actually enhance and

42

strengthen the prophetic message, for music and prophecy have a close and continuing relationship.

# Chapter 4
# The Role of Music

In the Word of God there is a close association between music and prophecy. The Scriptures contain many references which deal with this close relationship between music and prophecy, and many prophetic songs are to be found in both the Old and the New Testaments.

We know, of course, that music is a powerful tool, and that music is part of the essential nature of the believer, for we have already noted Paul's exhortations on singing (*see* Ephesians 5:18,19; Colossians 3:16), which suggest that the presence of the Spirit in the believer also means the presence of music in the believer. To be filled with the Spirit is to be filled with song. The Spirit is a singing Spirit, and therefore we can expect Him to give us songs and to speak through us in song.

Many biblical revelations were first delivered musically; at times Old Testament prophets sang their prophecies instead of speaking them as God moved upon them and gave them spontaneous words and melodies. (It is important to remember the melodies these prophets sang were not in the scales or modes we are most familiar with in the Western Hemisphere. Many such prophecies are found in the books we call the major and minor prophets. Of the major prophets, Isaiah probably prophesied in song quite frequently. Throughout the book of Isaiah we find the word "burden"—for example, 13:1, "The burden of Babylon," or 14:28, "In the year that king Ahaz died was this burden." The word "burden" comes from the Hebrew word *massa,* meaning an utterance, primarily of doom, and especially with singing—prophecy in song. Other examples of Isaiah's songs of prophecy can be found in chapters 3, 15, 16, 17, 19, 21, 22, 23, and 30.

We find this word "burden," or prophetic song, used in the other prophetic books as well. God spoke to Ezekiel and told him, "Say thou unto them, Thus saith the Lord GOD; This burden concerneth the prince in Jerusalem, and all the house of Israel that are among them" (Ezekiel 12:10). The prophet Nahum spoke of "the burden of Nineveh" (Nahum 1:1), and Habakkuk wrote of "the burden which Habakkuk the prophet did see" (Habakkuk 1:1). Similar prophetic songs are recorded in Zechariah 9:1 and 12:1 and in Malachi 1:1.

It is interesting that many of the choruses we sing today come from the major and minor prophets. There is a musical anointing upon these books because the Word of God was sent forth on the wings of melody. They cry out to be sung with musical accompaniment, for they were birthed with melody by the Holy Spirit.

### Jubal—The First Musician

The first mention of music in the Scriptures is found in Genesis 4 with the introduction of Jubal, the chief instructor of those who played the wind and stringed instruments. "And his [Jabal's] brother's name was Jubal: he was the father of all such as handle the harp and organ" (Genesis 4:21). Not much is said about Jubal in this one verse; however, much is contained in his name. Hebrew names were often prophetic, pointing to what the person would be or do. In fact, it was common to refrain from naming a child at birth but to wait until the child had developed to a point where some idea could be had of his personality and nature, and then to name him accordingly. Jubal's name contains insight into the man and his musical abilities, for his name means "a stream; to flow, to bring forth with pomp, to carry, to lead forth." A musician has the ability to bring forth a stream—a flow. It comes from within him, from the Spirit within him. So Jubal, by his name and nature [musical ability] set the stage for the ministry of musicians from then on. Out of the flow that comes from the Spirit within, today's Jubals can lead forth in prophetic songs.

## Prophetic Music in the Old Testament

Throughout the Old Testament there are recorded prophecies which came forth musically. We are familiar with Moses' great song of victory after the children of Israel were miraculously led across the Red Sea and the Egyptian forces were drowned in those same waters. Notice that the song of rejoicing became a prophetic utterance as Moses proclaimed what would happen as a result of that victory: "The people shall hear, and be afraid: sorrow shall take hold on the inhabitants of Palestine. Then the dukes of Edom shall be amazed; the mighty men of Moab, trembling shall take hold upon them; all the inhabitants of Canaan shall melt away. Fear and dread shall fall upon them; by the greatness of thine arm they shall be as still as a stone; till thy people pass over, O LORD, till the people pass over, which thou hast purchased. Thou shalt bring them in, and plant them in the mountain of thine inheritance, in the place, O LORD, which thou hast made for thee to dwell in, in the Sanctuary, O LORD, which thy hands have established" (Exodus 15:14-17). What a pronouncement!

Samuel spoke of music in connection with prophecy when he foretold events to come in the life of Saul. He told Saul, "Thou

47

shalt meet a company of prophets coming down from the high place with a psaltery, and a tabret, and a pipe, and a harp, before them; and they shall prophesy'' (1 Samuel 10:5). These prophets were coming from a garrison of Philistines that protected a place of idolatry—for "high places" in Scripture almost always were places where idols were worshipped—and yet in spite of that, they were worshipping. And they must have been singing! They carried musical instruments in their hands. We are not told if they were singing their prophecies or accompanying the prophetic words with musical praise, but I believe these prophets knew how to prophesy in song with their voices and with their instruments. They no doubt praised the Lord often, and as God was manifested in their praises, the prophetic unction would rise within them and they would speak forth divinely-inspired words.

It is likely that one who attended the "school of the prophets" in those days was required to have some type of musical training. The Scripture we have just read says that a psaltery (a bottle-shaped harp, or a "lyre," NIV), a tabret (a percussion instrument that was shaken—a "tambourine," NKJV), a pipe (a single- or double-tubed perforated flute), and a harp were with the prophets as they traveled—in fact, were "before them." This implies that these instruments were in front of the prophets, or in their hands. We can assume that these prophets were skilled in the use of these instruments and understood the powerful effect of music combined with the prophecy.

David Blomgren states that "the schools of the prophets instructed not only in the Law and the Scriptures but also in singing, especially psalm-singing. Eusebius, known as the father of church history, stated that the instruction in the school of the prophets was done by riddles, proverbs, and chanting of sacred and secular poems and by singing songs. Sendrey, a Jewish scholar, says that it is undeniable that the 'sons of the prophets' received systematic

48

and thorough instruction in music."[1]

Music prepares hearts to receive the word of the Lord, and the musical praise that these prophets no doubt expressed "set the stage" for the word of the Lord. So music can either prepare the way for the prophetic word, or it can be the channel for the prophecy itself. Either way, the music is an important element.

Elisha also knew the importance of music in receiving and flowing in the prophetic anointing. When he was sought out by Jehoshaphat to bring a word from God in a time of crisis, he instructed the men to "bring me a minstrel. And it came to pass, when the minstrel played, that the hand of the LORD came upon him [Elisha]. And he said, Thus saith the LORD..." (2 Kings 3:15,16). The minstrel played, and the music created an atmosphere in which God could dwell. God dwells in the praises of His people (Psalm 22:3). What makes the ministry of music so powerful is when God not only dwells in our music but through our music speaks a prophetic word.

**The Ministry of Musicians**

The Old Testament is full of references to music and musicians and to the part they had in the life and worship of the children of Israel. We have already seen the time when one of their battles was fought not by the armies but by the musicians (*see* 2 Chronicles 20), and we know that music was an intimate part of their worship, from the day when Miriam led the singing and dancing in celebration of the release from the Egyptians, through the time when David danced before the Lord as the Ark returned, and in the dedication of the temple when the musicians lifted their songs and praises as one voice and the glory of the Lord descended in such a tremendous way.

David, of course, understood the importance of music and gave special attention to the place of music in the house of the Lord.

In his music department the musicians were given "waivers" from other duties to concentrate upon their ministry of music. Part of their daily responsibilities was to study and practice to sing with a prophetic anointing. Perhaps they spent hours singing unto the Lord in His presence.

One man was specially selected to instruct in this musical field. "Chenaniah, leader of the Levites in singing, was put in charge of carrying the ark and lifting up song. He instructed about these matters, because he was skilled and able" (1 Chronicles 15:22, Amplified Bible). The New King James Version says that he was "instructor in charge of the music, because he was skillful." We can assume that he had prophetic ability as well as musical skill, since we know that the musicians functioned in prophecy. As teacher and leader of the others, he was responsible to instruct both by word and by example, and all were to excel in music and in the anointing.

Two hundred eighty-eight talented singers were selected and trained in flowing in the prophetic realm, and they led the remaining four thousand. We are told that "David and the captains of the host separated to the service of the sons of Asaph, and of Heman, and of Jeduthun, who should prophesy with harps, with psalteries, and with cymbals: and the number of the workmen according to their service was: Of the sons of Asaph...which prophesied according to the order of the king. Of Jeduthun: the sons of Jeduthun...who prophesied with a harp, to give thanks and to praise the LORD. Of Heman...all these were the sons of Heman the king's seer in the words of God, to lift up the horn. All these were under the hands of their father for song in the house of the LORD, with cymbals, psalteries, and harps, for the service of the house of God....So the number of them, with their brethren that were instructed in the songs of the LORD, even all that were cunning ['skillful,' NKJV], was two hundred fourscore and eight"

(1 Chronicles 25:1-7).

## The Place of Instruments

There are many other examples that could be given. Usually we find references to both singers and those who played some type of musical instrument. We will discuss the subject of prophecy with instruments at more length in another chapter, but obviously the instruments had an important role in the music and in the prophetic flow; as we will see, prophecy sometimes comes forth by means of the instruments, so that the musicians playing the instruments are not just accompanying the singing but are in themselves a part of the prophetic ministry. The instruments help express and demonstrate the prophecy, so that the instrumental playing and the song may seem almost inseparable—the message being communicated would be incomplete without both.

The Scriptures we have just read from 1 Chronicles 25 clearly state that some of the appointed musicians prophesied on the harp and other instruments. The song of the Lord that came forth at the cleansing of the Temple began with trumpets and instruments (*see* 2 Chronicles 29:27). The Word of God was communicated in song upon the instruments; there were no lyrics, and yet there was still a message communicated and a spiritual attitude conveyed. An impression was given. God was heard playing through the musician.

Many of the songs recorded in Scripture were sung to the accompaniment of musical instruments. In several instances, just the playing of the musical instrument brought the prophetic anointing. The hand of God came upon Elisha as a result of the playing of the stringed instrument. Elisha understood the relationship of music to the prophetic realm, so he called for a minstrel to play. As a result, Elisha prophesied.

I praise God that musicians are numbered among those who

51

prophesy. Singers and players of instruments may sing the prophetic song, as may those in the congregation. It is a ministry no longer looked down upon as insignificant, unimportant, or even improper. As the prophets of old lifted up their voices and declared the word of God with melody, so we, too, can sing the prophetic word of the Lord. "For the prophecy came not in old time by the will of man: but holy men of God spake [or sang] as they were moved by the Holy Ghost" (2 Peter 1:21).

## Music Touches the Spiritual Realm

It is remarkable how we struggle with the concept of God singing and playing through His worshippers, but we do not seem to have trouble believing or accepting the opposite—that evil spirits can so possess someone that they can at times be heard speaking or singing through a person.

When I was in Haiti I became aware of the reality of the kingdom of darkness and how it so perversely imitates the truths of the kingdom of God's marvelous light. Lying upon my bed at night, I could hear the distant throb of voodoo drums as the musicians called upon the spirits of darkness and invited them to draw nearer so the worshippers could know their presence.

It has been reported that in the midst of voodoo worship, after hours of demon-inspired singing, there would come a time when one of the worshippers possessed by evil spirits would stop singing a recognizable song and would begin to sing a song never heard before. It was understood that at that time the spirit possessing the person was singing. The song would reach a new climactic crescendo. The music of the worshipping musicians was of utmost importance in producing this state. Music touches the supernatural and releases spiritual activity, and for that reason music is integrally linked to the prophetic realm.

One of the secrets in reaching this spiritual state is total abandonment. Friends of mine who have encountered this type of activity have told me of seeing a human being actually suspended in the air from six to ten feet above the ground and being held there for several minutes by the strength of the evil forces within. If such things are not only possible but actual, why should it be so difficult to believe that the Holy Spirit, Who is infinitely more powerful than any demon, would bring forth prophetic manifestations through a musician who is yielded to the Lord Jesus Christ?

Music is one of mankind's fundamental avenues of communication, and one of the most successful because it transcends the conscious mind and reaches the subconscious. Music can bypass the gate that guards the entrance to the mind (which constantly tries to reduce the Word of God to what it can understand) and comes in another way. Music is "heart to heart," "spirit to spirit." That is why it is so destructive when used for evil. It touches the inner man. Music can work to our advantage or to our disadvantage, so we must always be careful what we sing. Music is not an appendage or a spare tire; it's a basic element of our worship.

### The Music of David

We know that David, the "sweet singer of Israel," was a prophet of God. "Now these be the last words of David. David the son of Jesse said, and the man who was raised up on high, the anointed of the God of Jacob, and the sweet psalmist of Israel, said, The Spirit of the LORD spake by me, and his word was in my tongue" (2 Samuel 23:1,2). Throughout the historical record and then in the book of Psalms, we find many of the songs that David composed and sang. Many were prophetic in nature; the major theme in these prophecies was the coming Messiah. As a matter of fact, there are over a dozen prophetic references to the Messiah in the book of Psalms, all of which are fulfilled in the New

53

Testament. David the singer was also David the worshipper, who prophesied in his music. Music is an integral part of worship, and so it was, and is, a channel of prophecy as well.

When we think of the Psalms we think of David, but he was not the only psalmist. The collection of songs we call the book of Psalms was written during a lengthy period ranging from the time of Moses to the post-exilic era of the second Temple. While David was the major contributor to this songbook, having written seventy-three of the psalms, others also added their inspired words: Asaph, who wrote twelve psalms; the sons of Korah, who wrote ten; Solomon, who wrote two; and Moses, Heman, and Ethan, who each wrote one psalm. These are all part of the divinely-inspired Word of God, and they are a beautiful example of prophecy in music.

## Music in the Prophetic Books

Many other prophecies found in the Old Testament were no doubt delivered in song. Isaiah frequently spoke forth the word of the Lord by singing, and many of those prophetic utterances are found in his book; in fact, many of the choruses we sing today come from the book of Isaiah. Ezekiel was another prophet who probably sang a number of his prophecies. In addition to these, some of the minor prophets used music as a way of expressing the messages God gave them to proclaim. Habakkuk delivered a prophetic prayer, "a prayer of Habakkuk the prophet upon Shigionoth" (Habakkuk 3:1) "to the chief singer on my stringed instruments" (verse 19). "Shigionoth" was a type of musical expression, perhaps indicating a piece of music that was passionately or wildly lyrical. This is harmonious with the form and content of this chapter, which indicates the intimate connection between music and prophecy.[2]

54

## Prophetic Music Is Contemporary

The same prophetic mantle that rested upon David and the other biblical musicians and songwriters can rest upon musicians and songwriters today. The same prophetic flow into which they entered is available in this present hour. All across the country I have heard musicians singing prophetic songs. One of the most powerful anthems of praise I have heard come forth with a prophetic anointing in the midst of a congregation is the song "All Hail, King Jesus." It can lift you into realms of praise and worship that you will never forget.

There is no other way that the zeal of the Lord is so expressed and so evident as in song. We need to recognize that in our church services we should not think of "first singing and then preaching," as though the two had nothing in common, but that there should be a continuous flow as we enter into the presence of God. God doesn't speak just through the pastor as he delivers his sermon; His words can be going forth as those new songs are sung.

I have a great desire to see more Christian musicians "tap into" this prophetic flow and bring forth words of the Spirit. There are thousands of individual musicians and groups who see their music as an evangelistic tool—and praise the Lord for the people who are hearing the Gospel message through music—but what about the many believers who need the exhortation, edification, and comfort that comes through the prophetic word? The ministry of music is not entertainment, and it is far more than just reaching the unsaved. God wants to speak through His musicians. He wants them to play and sing those new, spontaneous songs of praise and worship and to bring forth His words. He dwells in the praises of His people, and we will become aware of the prophetic flow as we move in those realms of praise.

# Chapter 5
# The Role of Praise

It is significant that praise and song are virtually inseparable. *Webster's New World Dictionary* tells us that one meaning of the verb "praise" is "to laud the glory of [God], *as in song*" (emphasis added). As we will see shortly, one of the major Old Testament words for "praise" has a musical definition. Praise is not always expressed in song, but singing our praise is mentioned more than three hundred times in the Bible—more than any other method of expressing praise or worship. Given this tie between them, it is to be expected that praise and the prophetic song also have a close relationship.

Hundreds of times throughout the Scriptures, particularly in the Psalms, we are exhorted to praise the Lord. "Praise ye the LORD. Praise, O ye servants of the LORD, praise the name of the LORD. Blessed be the name of the LORD from this time forth and for evermore. From the rising of the sun unto the going down of the same the LORD'S name is to be praised" (Psalm 113:1-3). In fact, the whole last segment of the book of Psalms deals with praise to God, and concludes, "Praise ye the LORD. Praise God in his sanctuary: praise him in the firmament of his power. Praise him for his mighty acts: praise him according to his excellent greatness. Praise him with the sound of the trumpet: praise him with the psaltery and harp. Praise him with the timbrel and dance: praise him with stringed instruments and organs. Praise him upon the loud cymbals: praise him upon the high sounding cymbals. Let every thing that hath breath praise the LORD. Praise ye the LORD'' (Psalm 150). What an all-encompassing picture of praise!

Because there are so many, many verses in Psalms on the subject of praise, we may tend to think that praise is Davidic. But praise is Divine. We are following God's pattern, not man's, when we praise. Praise is God's idea, God's command, and also God's pleasure. He loves to hear His people praising Him!

### Judah

Praise is first found in the Bible in Genesis 29:35, which is the account of the birth of Judah. Leah, his mother, was ''hated,'' according to the Scriptures, for she had become Jacob's wife through the deceit of Laban and had never been accepted or loved by Jacob. God gave her three sons, which she hoped would bring her the favor and love of her husband. She was totally involved with her children and the cherished hope of what they would do for her marriage. But when the fourth son arrived, she finally turned her attention from her family to her God, and said, ''Now I will praise the LORD: therefore she called his name Judah.'' This fourth son came from the ''joining'' that Leah declared had been accomplished (verse 34). Judah was a forebear of David, and through that lineage the Messiah came. No matter where Judah appears in the Scriptures, the name always means ''praise.''

When Judah had grown into a tribe, that tribe was always the first to pack up and move when the Israelites moved during their wilderness wanderings. Once the cloud had lifted and moved, Judah struck camp and moved also, followed by the two closest tribes;

then came the Tabernacle. When a new campsite was reached, Judah pitched their tents first, and the Tabernacle was reassembled and placed just east of their banner. Judah was closest to the place where God dwelt!

Judah figured significantly in the history of Israel. They led in the conquest of Canaan (*see* Judges 1:1-19); it was Judah whom God sent to combat gross sin in the tribe of Benjamin (*see* Judges 20); Judah was the first to make David king, and remained loyal to him in spite of rebellion (*see* 2 Samuel 2,20); and when the kingdom was divided, Judah became the leader of the Southern Kingdom (*see* 2 Kings 14:21,22).

We find Judah mentioned not only in the Pentateuch and the historical books but in the Psalms as well. It is also significant that Judah is mentioned more than 290 times in the prophetic books alone—reinforcing the relationship of praise to the prophetic utterance.

But praise is not confined to Scriptural references or concepts. In everyday life, people praise. If you don't think so, just watch a few television commercials; each company praises its product as being the newest, the greatest, the best—certainly better than its competitors! We praise things, abilities, other people, and even the dog when he learns to sit up or roll over. Surely, then, if everyday things rate praise, how much more should we be involved with praise of the God of heaven and earth!

## The Importance of Praise

As we have read in Psalms 113 and 150, God has told us that we are to praise Him. It is His will for His children. Over and over again in the Scriptures we are exhorted to praise and instructed in praise. It is God's will and command.

Let us look at Psalm 81 to get a good picture of praise and its importance. Verse 1 tells us, "Sing aloud unto God our strength:

59

make a joyful noise unto the God of Jacob." (This gets both singers and non-singers in on the act!) Verse 2 includes the musicians: "Take a psalm, and bring hither the timbrel, the pleasant harp with the psaltery." No one is excluded, whether "musical" or not! The key is in verse 4. "For this was a statute for Israel, and a law of the God of Jacob." Praise is not an activity for a few select ones. As Corrie ten Boom has said, "God's Word contains no suggestions—only commands." Verse 1 of Psalm 81 does not suggest that it might be a good thing if we could get around to perhaps offering praise to the Lord. It tells us to do it! Praise is a **command.**

All God's creation, from the lowest to the highest, sings praise to Him. "Sing, O ye heavens; for the LORD hath done it: shout, ye lower parts of the earth: break forth into singing, ye mountains, O forest, and every tree therein" (Isaiah 44:23). His created beings are praisers: "Praise ye him, all his angels: praise ye him, all his hosts" (Psalm 148:2). The sun, moon, and stars offer praise, for "the heavens declare the glory of God; and the firmament sheweth his handiwork" (Psalm 19:1); they are told, "Praise ye him, sun and moon; praise him, all ye stars of light" (Psalm 148:3). Nature itself is instructed to praise the Lord: "Let the heavens rejoice, and let the earth be glad; let the sea roar, and the fulness thereof. Let the field be joyful, and all that is therein: then shall all the trees of the wood rejoice before the LORD" (Psalm 96:11-13a). "Praise the LORD from the earth, ye dragons, and all deeps: fire, and hail; snow, and vapours; stormy wind fulfilling his word: mountains, and all hills; fruitful trees, and all cedars: beasts, and all cattle; creeping things, and flying fowl" (Psalm 148:7-10). We are even told that "surely the wrath of man shall praise thee (Psalm 76:10). If all the lesser ranks of God's creation praise Him, how can man, the highest of God's creation, do anything else!

Praise is not a choice; it is a command. It is not optional; it is obligatory. It is not a privilege; it is a prerequisite. Not to praise is to be disobedient to a specific command of God. Jesus said, "If ye love me, keep my commandments" (John 14:15). If we fail at this point, how then can we say that we love God, or continue in His ways?

One of the most frequently sung songs in all of Christendom sums it up: "Praise God, from Whom all blessings flow. Praise Him, all creatures here below; praise Him above, ye heavenly host; praise Father, Son, and Holy Ghost!" Amen! So be it!

In verse 5 of Psalm 81, we find that praise is a **testimony**: "This he ordained in Joseph for a testimony." Praise speaks forth wondrous things of God and His ways. "And he hath put a new song in my mouth, even praise unto our God; many shall see it, and fear, and shall trust in the LORD" (Psalm 40:3). Praise brings God-consciousness. The testimony of God is not His power but His praise! Our praises show God to the world. Where there are praising believers, God is the center of attention because He is the Source and the Object of that praise.

Peter declared that we "are a chosen generation, a royal priesthood, an holy nation, a peculiar people; that ye should shew forth the praises of him who hath called you out of darkness into his marvellous light" (1 Peter 2:9). We are called to be witnesses unto Him (*see* Acts 1:8). We have been "chosen...in him before the foundation of the world...that we should be to the praise of his glory" (Ephesians 1:4,12). He is lifted up for all to see and adore when we offer praise to Him.

Praise is also a **deliverance**. "I removed his shoulder from the burden: his hands were delivered from the pots. Thou calledst in trouble, and I delivered thee" (Psalm 81:6,7). There is a power in praise that can bring deliverance, as we noticed earlier in this book when talking about the results of the prophetic song. God dwells in praise; the all-powerful and all-knowing One, Who has never experienced loss or defeat, resides there, so no adversary has a chance. After their deliverance from the Egyptians, Moses and the children of Israel sang, "Who is like unto thee, O LORD, among the gods? who is like thee, glorious in holiness, fearful in praises, doing wonders? (Exodus 15:11). Victory is certain and prevailing power is present when praises are sung. We're no longer slaves; we're free! The Lion of the tribe of Judah [praise] has prevailed over all our enemies!

Praise also brings deliverance from mourning, depression, and a heavy spirit. The Spirit of God singing in man will cause one to be uplifted. Discouragement or depression can be dispelled as praises are offered to God. The result is as sure as God's promises. "Therefore the redeemed of the LORD shall return, and come with singing unto Zion; and everlasting joy shall be upon their head: they shall obtain gladness and joy; and sorrow and mourning shall flee away" (Isaiah 51:11).

The prophetic word given through Isaiah was "the Spirit of the Lord GOD is upon me; because...he hath sent me...to appoint unto them that mourn in Zion, to give unto them beauty for ashes, the oil of joy for mourning, the garment of praise for the spirit of heaviness" (Isaiah 60:1,3). The Christian living in Zion (God's presence) is to be clothed in the garment of praise. This article of spiritual clothing is most miraculous, for when the believer is wearing it, the principle of cause and effect goes into operation. When he puts it on, the spirit of heaviness immediately departs. Depression, weighty spirits, heavy burdens, and accompanying worries fall away when praise begins. The Spirit of God sings accolades to the Father as the believer begins to vocalize what is stirring in his heart and his inner eyes look to the Almighty. His consciousness of the mundane, the ordinary, and the problem-laden realm fades as he begins to soar in heavenly places. Regenerated man was not meant to roost on the earth like a chicken;

he is destined to mount up with wings as an eagle. Chickens don't fly; they flutter and sputter, with insignificant results. But eagles soar with very little effort as they catch the updrafts of air. So the "eagle" Christian can soar on wings of praise, with very little striving, and rise on the updrafts of the Spirit of God. From this high and lofty position he is not overwhelmed with the heaviness of life but finds himself overcoming it in praise.

The Christian who "mounts up with wings as eagles" is the one who has learned to "wait upon the Lord" (*see* Isaiah 40:31). As he confidently expects God to come, he exchanges his strength for God's. Waiting does not mean total passivity, lying around doing nothing. The Bible says, "Praise waiteth for thee, O God, in Sion: and unto thee shall the vow be performed" (Psalm 65:1). In the presence of God (Zion), saints are participating in praise and expecting the Lord to do what He has promised. In other words, they who wait, praise.

But simply singing praise is not enough. The Bible tells us we are to "sing praises to God, sing praises: sing praises unto our King, sing praises. For God is the King of all the earth: sing ye praises with *understanding*" (Psalm 47:6,7, emphasis added). God wants us to understand the principles of praise and the cause and effects of offering the sacrifice of praise. We are to praise with an understanding of what we are doing and why we are doing it.

## Understanding Praise

Every church or denomination has its own definition of praise or manifestation of what it believes praise to be. To some, praise means singing a few lively choruses; to others, praising God is singing quiet, unhurried songs of thanksgiving or adoration. Some may say, "Hallelujah, praise the Lord" once or twice and feel that they have praised God. What does the Bible say to us about praise?

Several Hebrew words are translated "praise" in the King James Version of the Old Testament. One of these is *tehillah* (or *tehilloh*), which can be defined as "laudations or hymns of the Spirit." A *tehillah* is a song sung in the Spirit, a new song sung spontaneously to the Lord, or chants sung when praying or praising. This is an important word in our understanding of praise and the role of praise in the prophetic song. In fact, the book of Psalms is known as the book of *Tehillum*. It is a book of songs sung by the Holy Spirit through David, Asaph, the sons of Korah, and others. Within this word is the suggestion of God singing through us, or at least giving a song within to be sung as the inspiration rises.

Let us look at some of the Scriptures that contain this word *tehillah* and see the application. For instance, Psalm 22:3, which is a prophetic song played and sung by David, says, "But thou art holy, O thou that inhabitest the praises of Israel." This tells us that God dwells in *tehillah*—in the laudations of the Holy Spirit within us. *Tehillah* is His habitat. He manifests His localized presence in this praise. (This is not the same as His omnipresence.) When praise arises, it creates an atmosphere in which God can dwell. Praise is the atmosphere of heaven, and when God finds that same atmosphere here, in our praises, it is familiar—it is not foreign to Him or adverse to His nature—so He comes to dwell in it.

A well-known Scripture that we often quote, and often misunderstand, is Psalm 100:4—"Enter into his gates with thanksgiving, and into his courts with praise." I often thought that as I sang a chorus or hymn I was entering His presence. But this may not necessarily be so. The Word of God says that *tehillah* is the entrance to His courts. Notice Isaiah 60:18, in which the prophet said, "...thou shalt call thy walls Salvation, and thy gates Praise." Isaiah said that we pass through the gates to enter Zion by means of our songs of praise. Zion is where God dwells. "For the LORD hath chosen Zion; he hath desired it for his habitation.

This is my rest for ever: here will I dwell; for I have desired it" (Psalm 132:13,14). The Ark of the Covenant was in Zion. Above the Mercy Seat, between the wings of the cherubim, was a manifestation of God's presence (*see* Exodus 25:22). So God is telling us that we can come into His presence (Zion) with *tehillah*. It is the gate that leads to the King's courts.

The Scriptures from Psalm 132 that we have just read tell us that God chose Zion for His dwelling place because He desired to abide there. We are told further that "The LORD loveth the gates of Zion more than all the dwellings of Jacob" (Psalm 87:2). God loves our praise. He delights in the spontaneous outpourings of our hearts to Him. "Praise is comely for the upright" (Psalm 33:1b). "Praise ye the LORD: for it is good to sing praises unto our God; for it is pleasant; and praise is comely" (Psalm 147:1).

The word "comely" can be defined as "appropriate, becoming, or suitable." Praise, including spontaneous singing in the Spirit, is appropriate for believers. The glow of God's presence as His children praise Him is very becoming to them. "Out of Zion, the perfection of beauty, God hath shined" (Psalm 50:2). As Moses' face shone with the glory of God, so the shine of God's presence will be upon the faces of those who spend time in His presence praising and worshipping Him. The Almighty will shine forth out of Zion. His glory will be revealed in the countenances and lives of those who have been close to Him, for they will radiate God to the world. Their lives will emit the fragrance of His presence, causing others to realize that they have been with Him. The light of His glory cannot be hidden. "Arise, shine; for thy light is come, and the glory of the LORD is risen upon thee. For, behold...the LORD shall arise upon thee, and his glory shall be seen upon thee. And the Gentiles shall come to thy light, and kings to the brightness of thy rising...they shall shew forth the praise of the LORD" (Isaiah 60:1-3,6b).

Isaiah also records God's declaration that "mine house shall be called a house of prayer for all people" (56:7). The word for prayer is the Hebrew word *tephillah*, which is very similar to the word *tehillah* which we have just seen. God wants His house to be a place where prayers are sung as well as spoken. He wants the Church to be known for singing prayers and praise. It's both interesting and significant to notice how many forms of our communion with God involve music.

The Church is not a building; it is a body of believers who congregate for a common purpose. The very focal point of what God is doing in music is found in the Church—the assembling of the saints. It is in the midst of this assembly, as praises ascend to heaven, that God dwells. Psalm 114:2 tells us that "Judah was his sanctuary." Praise was the place where God was to be found. "But thou art holy, O thou that inhabitest the praises of Israel" (Psalm 22:3). God lives in the praises of His people. He takes up residence in the midst of His people as they sacrifice to Him. In Old Testament days the people offered sacrifices of animals or birds when they came to God. Today we offer sacrifices of joy, thanksgiving, righteousness, praise—and God comes to dwell in them.

We are told, "By him therefore let us offer the sacrifice of praise to God continually, that is, the fruit of our lips giving thanks to his name" (Hebrews 13:15). We are also told, "I [God] create the fruit of the lips" (Isaiah 57:19). God is the source of the sacrifice of praise that we are to offer unto Him. As we offer this sacrifice of praise unto Him, there comes a time when it is no longer us praising or singing, but it is the Holy Spirit singing through us.

God wants us to "make his praise glorious" (Psalm 66:2). As we sing to Him, and He sings through us, His *tehillah* can become tremendously spectacular and awesome. It will be shown forth in all the earth. David declared, "His *tehillah* shall continually be in my mouth" (Psalm 34:1), and according to Joel 3:20, "Judah [praise] shall dwell (Hebrew "abide") forever." Though praise may be expressed in a variety of ways, it can and should be ever present, for "his praise (*tehillah*) endureth for ever" (Psalm 111:10).

### "Joyful" Praise

The Scriptures, particularly the Psalms, describe many kinds of praise. David and the other psalmists speak often of rejoicing and of expressing praise to God in an exuberant or demonstrative manner. "Praise ye the LORD. I will praise the Lord with my whole heart" (Psalm 111:1). This certainly suggests that the praising was done with enthusiasm and vigor! Raising our hands, clapping our hands, or dancing before the Lord—all of which are not only endorsed but commanded in Scripture—are all demonstrations of our inner feelings being released in praise to God.

Quite often praisers are criticized for being "too emotional" or "too loud," but the Bible says, "Let the children of Zion be joyful in their King" (Psalm 149:3); "blessed is the people that know the joyful sound" (Psalm 89:15). The Hebrew word for "joyful" actually means "earsplitting." How many of us have ever even come close to that level in our praising!

I don't find scriptural references to praise being sung or played quietly. The sound of God seems to be a loud sound! "God is gone up with a shout" (Psalm 47:5), the psalmist declared.

At the time of the rebuilding of the Temple, we find that "when the builders laid the foundation of the temple of the LORD, they set the priests in their apparel with trumpets, with the Levites the sons of Asaph with cymbals, to praise the LORD, after the ordinance of David king of Israel. And they sang together by course in praising and giving thanks unto the LORD; because he is good, for his mercy endureth for ever toward Israel. And all the people shouted with a great shout, when they praised the LORD, because the foundation of the house of the LORD was laid....for the people shouted with a loud shout, and the noise was heard afar off" (Ezra 3:10,11,13). The people "shouted aloud for joy," the record tells us, and their singing and praising was heard for miles around. Talk about a praise service! All their neighbors knew that God's people were praising Him!

When the heavens were opened to John and he beheld what was happening at the throne of God, he said of the One Whom he saw, "His voice [was] as the voice of many waters" (Revelation 1:15). Interestingly, he used this same description when recording the sound made by those who were singing and playing before the Throne: "And I heard a voice from heaven, as the voice of many waters, and as the voice of a great thunder" (14:2); "and I heard as it were the voice of a great multitude, and as the voice of many waters, and as the voice of mighty thunderings, saying, Alleluia: for the Lord God omnipotent reigneth" (19:6). The Amplified Bible translates this verse "After that I heard what sounded like the shout of a vast throng, like the boom of many pounding waves and like the roar of terrific and mighty thunder-peals."

John compared the sound he heard to the sound of rushing water, or of pounding waves. Anyone who has been to Niagara Falls certainly remembers the roar made by those great waters as they fall so many hundreds of feet to the river below. Some say that all the sounds in the sound spectrum are found in the sound of crashing water. What John heard is what scientists call "white noise," which can be explained as "all frequencies sounding simultaneously." White noise is what is heard on the beach as the waves roll in and beat upon the shoreline in tremendous explosions of sound.

John heard this great roar and explosive, thundering wave of sound as the voices ascended in praise and worship of Almighty God, and as the harpists and other musicians played. What a force of sound! What a musical dynamic! One hundred forty-four thousand voices were blended together in a tremendous outpouring of sound. I have heard approximately fifty thousand people sing at a Billy Graham crusade in the Kingdome in Seattle, Washington, and was awed at the greatness of the sound of all those voices blended in musical expression. I cannot imagine almost three times that many voices singing glorious praise to the Father. It was a sound that was literally out of this world! Each voice was roaring forth a spontaneous expression of praise and worship to God as John beheld and listened. What a celebration!

Praise is the sound that fills heaven. God desires that the earth also be filled with praise—not the sound of a congregation singing hymn number such-and-such or the newest chorus on the overhead projector, but many voices of believers singing their own spontaneous song to God. John did not say that he heard one distinguishable melody or lyric, but he heard a great deafening outburst of praise as each individual voice blended with another to become a whole, forming one tremendous sound of praise.

The book of Revelation is full of praise, and the first verse tells us why: "The revelation of Jesus Christ...." When revelation of Jesus is received, praise and worship follow. When we truly see Jesus, we cannot help expressing the response of our hearts. Our voices join with millions in heaven to be part of that great sound as every knee bows and every tongue confesses that Jesus Christ is the Lord of lords and the King of kings. He is exalted above all gods; His name is above every name in heaven and on earth. He is the only Supreme Potentate. Every creature, every nation, and every person in every language will sing glorious, audible praise to our exalted Lord.

The Lord delights in the praise of His people, and He is

completely at home in their loud praises! We see in 1 Chronicles that when the Levites carried the Ark, "David told the chief Levites to appoint their brethren the singers with instruments of music, harps, lyres, and cymbals, to play loudly and lift up their voices with joy" (1 Chronicles 15:16, Amplified Bible). The Ark speaks to us of the presence of God. These musicians made a loud, joyful noise because God's presence was among them. When God's presence is manifested and we become aware of it, we too will become louder and more joyful in singing our praise!

This is not an endorsement of noise for its own sake, for there are some who make noise just to be obnoxious, or use God's commands as a license to become chaotic or to let their fleshly expressions take over. That is not praise. Praise is a sacrifice of thanksgiving and honor to the Lord. It is a declarative statement and must come from the heart. It must start with God and end with God, and speak of God in between.

## Praise and the Prophetic Song

Throughout this chapter we have constantly referred to the singing of praise—in fact, not making much distinction between the two because of their intimate relationship. Of course, we must understand that just because someone is singing does not necessarily mean he is praising. For singing to be praise, the one who is singing must be consciously singing **about** the Lord or **to** the Lord. Not every song is a song of praise; a true song of praise will be about Christ Himself or about what He has done. We must learn not to "sing into the air" but to be aware of the One about Whom and to Whom we are singing.

Hebrews 2:12 quotes Christ as saying, "I will declare thy name unto my brethren, in the midst of the church will I sing praise unto thee." The Greek word for "sing" is *humneo,* from which we get our word "hymn." It has the meaning of singing a religious ode, or celebrating God in song. If the type of singing Jesus does when praising is that which celebrates God, then that should be the type of singing we do when praising.

However, when we are talking about the prophetic song, our goal is to rise in praise to that song so that we experience the singing of the Lord. Singing from the intellect, or even from a soul response, is not the same as singing in the Spirit; we must move from a physical performance to a spirit response.

The book of Judges tells of an episode in Israel's history which involved Deborah and Barak. Following a significant victory, these two sang, "I, even I, will sing unto the LORD: I will sing praise to the LORD God of Israel" (Judges 5:3). As they sang their praise, they flowed right into a beautiful prophetic song.

Psalm 29 begins, "Give unto the LORD the glory due unto his name; worship the LORD in the beauty of holiness." Then verses three through nine speak of "the voice of the Lord" and what it produced. The praise was followed by God speaking. We, too, will find that in our praising we can "catch the wave," so to speak, and be borne higher until we touch that area of prophetic flow. Then it can be released through us in song. "Sing unto God...O sing praises unto the Lord...lo, he doth send out his voice, and that a mighty voice" (Psalm 68:32,33). The singing **about** the Lord and **to** the Lord becomes the singing **of** the Lord, and we hear His voice.

As the prophetic song comes forth in the congregation, it will immediately do three things. It will **unify** the congregation, for it will present one concept—perhaps the love of God for His people, or His faithfulness, or perhaps something He desires. But whatever the concept, it will bring a unification in the praising of the congregation, who may be praising in several different directions or on several different levels.

The prophetic song will give **direction** to the praise and worship expressions of the congregation. For instance, perhaps the singer will extol the majesty of God. This will help to bring the congregation to a place where all are moving in the same vein of expression, so that all are bringing forth expressions that reflect God's majesty.

A third effect of the prophetic song is to give **inspiration**. A song speaking of the imminent fulfillment of a promise of God, for example, would no doubt produce a great sense of joy among the people. This would inspire further and perhaps higher expressions of praise. Songs given by the Spirit usually lead the congregation into higher levels of worship.

**Singing the New Song**

In our praise—our *tehillah*—we sing by the inspiration of the Holy Spirit; to be more accurate, by the inspiration and empowering of the Spirit of God, He sings through us. The ministry of the Holy Spirit is to exalt the Lord Jesus and bring attention to Him. If we are overflowing with the Spirit, we will not find it difficult to sing *tehillah*. God puts that new song in our mouths. We can't even praise Him unless He gives us the words and the music, for He is the power that works in us to will and to do of His good pleasure. God implants the *tehillah*; we flow with the inspiration. He gives the new song; we sing with the Spirit. "Open thy mouth wide, and I will fill it" (Psalm 81:10), He told Israel. Though we know that His promise to the children of Israel was to fill their mouths with natural provision during their time in the wilderness, I believe we can be assured that if we open our mouths in praise to Him, He will fill them with His own words and music!

It is not unusual for a praiser to awaken during the night and be aware that the Spirit within him is praising the Lord in song. I believe it would not be unusual for this to happen during the day, too, if our conscious minds did not so firmly and rigidly

72

control our spirits.

The Spirit within us wants to release that new song. God delights in hearing it. But sometimes we just don't quite "let ourselves go." So often there is opposition within us in regard to this matter of lifting up our voice and singing praise to God. What we must understand is that the nature of God is different from ours, and that our natural self repels the things of God and desires that which is the opposite of God's nature. But the new man within us reaches out toward God and the things of God. So the opposition we sense and with which we struggle, in regard to God's purpose for musical praise and the directives He gives, comes from the conflict between the natural man and the spiritual man. Whenever our reaction is to squelch the expression of the Spirit, we are identifying with our old natures and not with God's Word.

Sometimes we're just plain afraid. I was, the first time I heard the sound of loud, free, spontaneous praise. But when I found out it was God's way, I crucified the fears and voices of my flesh and obeyed the Word of God. Once the spirit is released in this expression, there comes a great sense of pleasure. There is no greater joy, fulfillment, or satisfaction than that which is experienced in His presence. Truly "in thy presence is fulness of joy; at thy right hand there are pleasures for evermore" (Psalm 16:11). The pleasures of sin last for only a brief time; the pleasures one experiences in drawing near to God last for eternity. They are without end. There is no earthly "high" that can even begin to compare with just a moment in His presence when praise is flowing forth to Him.

Don't be afraid; be bold! Step out and sing unto the Lord. Release those new, spontaneous songs that the Lord gives. Offer *tehillah* to Him. If you have never done it before, it may seem strange at first, but remember that your mind cannot comprehend it, so let your spirit bypass your mind, and do it because God has said

73

that He enjoys it and wants you to do it! In fact, you can even put down this book right now, and before you continue reading, let the Spirit flow through you in expressions of musical praise unto God. Hallelujah! We praise You, Lord! We rejoice in You! We sing a new song to You!

The more we continue to flow in musical praise to Him, the more readily we will find ourselves aware of the presence of the spirit of prophecy and able to flow in the prophetic song. God gives it to us and through us, so we have a very important part to play—one that demands understanding and preparation.

# Chapter 6

# The Role of the Musician

When we understand that God has limited Himself to move through His people, we can understand that He expresses His song through us. Most often He directs His song through one skilled in the art of music, but He does not exclude other Christians, filled with the Spirit of God, who also can prophesy in song by the Holy Spirit. More often, however, it is the skilled musicians whom God calls to prophesy in song.

We have already read the Old Testament account of the appointment by David of musicians to praise and prophesy in music (*see* 1 Chronicles 25). The spiritual leadership set apart those who would flow in prophetic music. This was their job description. The musician was to be an oracle of God. He was not to evangelize, testify of personal experience, or entertain; his appointment was for the purpose of edifying and exhorting through music. Occasionally he would sing of future events.

We also know, from Ephesians 5:18 and Colossians 3:16, that we are to be filled with the Spirit and with the Word of God. Without these, we cannot sing spiritual songs. God is looking for musicians (and non-musicians) who are so filled with the Spirit and the Word (not with sense-altering stimuli) that they sing and play psalms, hymns, and songs of the Spirit of God—songs that are Spirit-inspired and Spirit-sung. Every Spirit-filled musician has the ability within him to bring forth "spiritual songs," whether he recognizes it or not, because the Spirit within him is a singing Spirit and desires to manifest the song of the Lord.

## Songs of the Spirit

Our study of the name of Jubal, the first musician, indicated that Jubal's name meant a stream, a bringing forth. That stream or flow comes from within the musician. In the natural, a musician can bring forth a flow of sustained sound. The Spirit-filled musician can bring forth a stream of the music of the Spirit of God. The songs he brings forth will not come from a soulish or natural realm. They will not be songs of the flesh—childish songs which are man-centered or full of self-pity or self-seeking.

A musician should never play a song by improvisation and call it a prophetic song, for it was initiated by the natural mind, not by the Spirit of God. Nor should a song be created out of feelings, whether emotional moods or responses of the senses, for then the song comes from the soul. The song must be the result of the Spirit rising within the musician. Therefore, there must be a certain level of maturity in the Spirit-led musician, for he must know the difference between the song that the Spirit of God would inspire and sing and the song which is naturally improvised (as in a "jam session").

Applying the meaning of Jubal's name—that of bringing forth a stream, with pomp and ceremony—to musicians in general, we can understand that any musician, whether saved or not, has the ability to bring forth a stream, with a showy display of splendor, pageantry, or magnificence that will greatly impress others who are not musical. The unsaved musician, skillful in his art, can be grandiose and splendid in showy display as he jumps, gyrates, and dances in front of the audience, playing music that stimulates the baser drives of man. A good example is music videos—often vulgar visual displays of the performer playing, singing, and dancing while special effects, creatures, and human bodies are arranged and choreographed to glorify death, darkness, and devils. Even if the musician calls himself a Christian, if he has not made Jesus Christ his Lord he will very likely bring forth that which is of the world, not that which is of God.

The Spirit-filled and Spirit-led musician is also to bring forth a stream with pomp, but his stream glorifies the Lord Jesus Christ. It is interesting to note that in both the Ephesians and the Colossians passages to which we have so often referred, the singing and melody are directed to the Lord—never to a person. There is no mention of audience rapport or response. The singer is to express his music with grace in his heart, according to the Colossians reference. He is not to sing in pride or self-exaltation. No singer should ever bring forth a song to impress people or cause them to respond to him personally. There is, of course, an appropriate appreciation of a gift or talent in an individual, but the song should lift up Jesus and direct all eyes to Him. If we sing to Him, people will follow us to Him.

The splendor which this musician puts on display is the splendor of God's magnificence. God's majesty and grandeur bring awe and response in the listener. This is the pomp today's Christian Jubals are to produce.

I see the Christian Jubals as floodgates of the rivers of God. When they are opened, streams of Divine life flow out to thirsty souls ready to drink in the waters of God's presence. It is not just one person; all the wells must spring forth, and all the floodgates must be opened! God declared, ''I will open rivers in high places, and fountains in the midst of valleys: I will make the wilderness a pool of water, and the dry land springs of water" (Isaiah 41:18). Ezekiel had a vision of "waters to swim in" and trees that produced new fruit because of the waters that "issued out of the sanctuary" (Ezekiel 47:5,12). The waters that come forth from the presence of God bring life-giving fruit!

As floodgates, we have the ability to bring forth or to hold back those waters. We can restrict the flood of God, or we can release it. If we choose not to release the song the Spirit gives, and hold it back behind the dam of unwillingness, the Spirit will not force us; but when we begin to release the river of the Holy Spirit in praise, the waters of God's presence will fill the Church—first to the ankles, and then to the knees, and then finally to the swimming point!—"and everything shall live whither the river cometh" (Ezekiel 47:9).

## Prophesying on Instruments

Earlier in this book, in our discussion of the role of music, we looked at a number of Scriptures that talked about the use of musical instruments in praising and prophesying. As we said then, prophecy sometimes comes forth on the instruments so that the musicians are not merely accompanying the singing but are themselves part of the prophetic flow. The instruments help demonstrate and express the prophecy.

The instrumental prophetic ministry was not haphazard. Both books of Chronicles speak of musical instruction. 1 Chronicles 25:7 notes that "their brethren...were instructed in the songs of the Lord," which certainly included instrumentalists, for verse 1 describes the men "who should prophesy with harps, with psalteries, and with cymbals." The account of the crowning of Joash as king speaks of "the singers with instruments of music, and such as taught to sing praise" (2 Chronicles 23:13).

The books of Chronicles abound with references to instruments and their use in singing and praising God. David set instrumentalists in place to praise and prophesy, and Solomon likewise had musicians with trumpets, cornets, psalteries, harps, and other instruments. The instruments were not an afterthought; they were a key element of the praise and the prophetic flow.

The word "prophesy" in 1 Chronicles 25:1 is the Hebrew word *naba*, which, as we have seen before, means "to prophesy, in speech or song, by inspiration (in prediction or simple discourse)." Obviously, when the Scripture says that the sons of Asaph and Heman and Jeduthan prophesied with instruments, it was not with speech but in song.

The key thing to notice here is that the [musical] prophecy comes by *inspiration*. When the spirit of prophecy is present and one is flowing in it, there is a sense of inspiration, or Divine impression. To be inspired is "to breathe in, or inhale." We breathe in the presence of God and exhale His thoughts in speech or song. One who has a Scripture can read it. One who has a word can speak it. One who has a song or melody can sing or play it and thereby exhale the Divine impression he sensed.

Prophecy testifies of Jesus, and our praise and worship must testify of the Lord Jesus Christ. The songs we sing and the music we play should testify of Jesus. All Scripture is given by inspiration of God (2 Timothy 3:16), so when we sing or play the Word of God, we are touching a prophetic expression.

The Bible says that "when ye come together, every one of you hath a psalm..." (1 Corinthians 14:26), which is "a sacred ode or cantillation, accompanied with harp or other instrument." The root word, *psallo*, has the meaning "to twang"—that is, to play on a stringed instrument. The emphasis here is on the instrument, not on the vocal expression. That verse goes on to say, "Let all things be done unto edifying." The instrument must be played in a manner that will edify. If the musician cannot discern in the

Spirit what is being played, he should not attempt to play.

You may be asking yourself, "How is it possible for a musician to prophesy on an instrument? Isn't prophecy a spoken message? How can it be prophecy if I don't hear words?"

Remember that when we are speaking of the prophetic song, we are not limiting that song to a **verbal** musical expression. It is true that the prophetic song will more often be sung in words; however, the musical accompaniment to that song—perhaps on a piano, or an organ, or a violin—is also a prophetic expression, for it is an enhancement to the words. It paints a picture. A vocal prophecy is often more effective when cloaked in beautiful music. It is like the difference between a black-and-white picture and one in vivid color. The music highlights the word but never distracts from it or overpowers it.

Prophecy on an instrument, whether melodic or chordal, is a Divine impression or revelation being played upon the instrument. It is a Holy Spirit-prompted song. There are several ways that a musician can step out in this expression. For instance, he can blend expressively with the prophetic message so that his music enhances the words. The goal is to add, to reinforce, to support or color, but never to bring attention to the musician or to supplant the message with the music. Another way is to play what has been sung or spoken in a different way; for example, if God has prophetically said that He will come as rain to His people, then the pianist could play in a manner that would depict water falling from heaven. "It takes some skill as a musician to make your instrument 'speak' in such a way."[1] What the instrument says should be a clear statement—a certain sound, bold and clear. "And even things without life giving sound, whether pipe or harp, except they give a distinction in the sounds, how shall it be known what is piped or harped?" (1 Corinthians 14:7).

Music is a language understood by all peoples, races, and

cultures. It transcends all philosophies, all theologies, all ideologies, all systems of belief. It touches the heart. God can use instruments for prophetic expression "to speak to His people who because of their prejudices and hurts are not able to hear through other means."[2] Instruments have always been very important in the prophetic ministry.

The musician can play the prophetic song on an instrument without accompanying lyrics or spoken message. God can speak supernaturally through a simple melody played on a clarinet by inspiration of the Holy Spirit. The melody makes a statement, paints a picture, leaves a Divine impression without the use of words. This is no less prophetic than any other prophetic expression.

Even the keyboard player or guitarist can make a prophetic statement without a melody line, just playing chords. The percussionist can prophesy on the trap set, congas or tympani, for it is the expression through the musician of the Divine inspiration he received that makes the music prophetic. It is still edifying though no words were uttered.

## The Musician Himself

If there is no musician, there is no musical expression; and if that musician is not prepared to flow in the prophetic song, God's message may be thwarted. Never should a musician be casual about it or take for granted that he can at any time or without prior thought or preparation be one who touches that Divine flow.

First and foremost, the musician who desires to enter the stream of God's Spirit and bring forth the prophetic song must be a worshipper of the Lord Jesus. His attention should be centered not on the song but on the One Who gives the song. He should actively seek Jesus—not service for Jesus, but Jesus Himself. We seek Him not for what He can do for us but for Who He is. To intimately know Him, to be close to Him and enjoy Him, is our most important goal. The first and greatest commandment is that we are to love the Lord our God with all our heart, soul, mind, and strength (*see* Mark 12:30,31)—to desire Him with all our heart, to enjoy Him with all our soul, to admire Him with all our mind, and to embrace Him with all our strength. To do less is to come short of God's purpose, desire, and command.

We know that "the Father seeketh such to worship him" (John 4:23). God is looking not for worship but for worshippers. He wants the person, not the form. The smell of the spices and the good ointments of our worship are pleasant to Him, but He would rather know the heart from which the worship comes. He wants the singer; then He will have the songs. He wants the player; then He will have the praise that comes when the instrument is played.

We must be what we sing. We are not perfected yet, but we must always endeavor to walk in the truth that we would minister. Failure to do this hinders the thrust of the message both in us and in those to whom it is given. In us, it may cause some doubt in our minds as we speak or sing the prophecy, thus diminishing the quality and the strength of the message as it is mixed with doubt and not with faith. Furthermore, since "to him who knoweth to do good, and doeth it not, to him it is sin" (James 4:17), if we are not obeying what we know God has spoken to us we are not in a position to hear from God. In others, the message can be hindered because they may sense that something is not quite right; though they may not know what it is, that awareness will affect their receptivity of the message.

When the Jews were living as captives in Babylon, they lamented, "By the rivers of Babylon, there we sat down, yea, we wept, when we remembered Zion. We hanged our harps upon the willows in the midst thereof. For there they that carried us away captive required of us a song; and they that wasted us required of us mirth, saying, Sing us one of the songs of Zion. How shall we sing the LORD'S song in a strange land?'' (Psalm 137:1-4). Away from Zion—out of the presence and dwelling place of God— there was no song. Nor can there be a spiritual song coming forth in our lives when we are separated from the place God wants us to be. If we are by the river of confusion, the only songs we will sing will be laments of our own miserable state. We must stay tapped into the river of God and experience the freshness that comes from Him. Without the Lord, our music is dry and dead; the well is dried up. He is our source of life and inspiration.

The heart and mind and spirit must be kept clean and pure unto God. The river of life that flows from the Throne of God must not be polluted or clogged by works of unrighteousness. "Who shall ascend into the hill of the LORD? or who shall stand in his holy place? He that hath clean hands, and a pure heart" (Psalm 24:3,4). Out of the heart flow the issues of life, and out of the, abundance of the heart the mouth speaks. If the musician is to bring forth a pure stream, his vessel must be clean. We are cleansed with the washing of water by the Word (*see* Ephesians 5:26), so time in the Word is absolutely essential for the believer who desires to sing the prophetic song.

Study of the Word is vital not only for the cleansing it supplies but for the understanding it brings. Any prophetic message must have its source in or be in agreement with the Word of God. Studying the Bible—not just reading a few little devotional lines every day—provides a broader base of understanding of the Kingdom of God, the principles of God, the ways of God, the acts of God, and even of the prophetic ministry itself. It is from this broad base that the Holy Spirit can bring to the believer's remembrance something he has read in the Scriptures and can breathe it through him in a prophetic song. "Let the Word of Christ dwell in you richly in all wisdom" so that spiritual songs can follow.

A musician will better prepare himself (or herself) for this ministry by spending time reading the scriptural accounts of singing unto the Lord, just as a preacher familiarizes himself with the patterns in God's Word before seeking inspiration for a sermon. "Extemporaneous" does not mean "unprepared"; it really means "drawing upon prior preparation" at a moment's notice. The more thorough that preparation is, the more complete the presentation will be. God's anointing is never an excuse for laziness. Somehow it seems that those who are the best prepared have the best anointing.

The Old Testament account of those who were appointed to play and sing the Lord's songs suggests that they were skillful in their art. I find it difficult to believe that God, in His perfect state, gives imperfect songs or is the Author of a sloppy melody. The problem lies with the musician. He may mentally hear a song that God is giving him but is unable to effectively present it because of his lack of skill and training, and so he stumbles and falters through the song, thus changing what was perfect in creation and inspiration into something mediocre. He could not musically interpret what he heard in the heavenlies because he had not spent time and energy in practice and preparation. The song that left the Father and was planted in his heart was therefore expressed in weakness and sloppiness, and the perfect became the mundane and ordinary—perhaps even the embarrassing. If that was our song, would we want to put our names on it? Let us be careful what we call "the song of the Lord."

God is perfect and excellent in His creative ability, and we are to express that kind of God to the world. Slothfulness, mediocrity, lethargy, and indifference have no place in the life of the Christian believer, let alone the Christian musician who desires to flow in the prophetic song. These are all opposed to what God is. Often Christians remain on the same musical plateau, creating and performing music which is so poor that it is a mockery of God. Excellence, integrity, high creativity, and a reaching toward perfection are qualities of God. These are to be in our music. How we play and sing tells the world what God is like.

None of us is perfect, of course, but we should all keep striving to improve and grow. We should seek for excellence in all things; and excellence is doing the best we can at the level where we are while reaching for higher levels.

### The Prophetic Song in Practice

Everything we have talked about in this book is for one primary purpose: to get us involved with actually singing the prophetic song. At this point, many will say, "Who? Me?" Yes, you!

Many are reluctant to actually become personally involved because they are afraid it will not be a true prophetic song. How can one know whether the song within is the song of the Lord, or just a song that was made up? This is a question that everyone who steps out in prophetic ministry must ask himself each time he flows in prophecy.

The Bible tells us, "Knowing this first, that no prophecy of the scripture is of any private interpretation. For the prophecy came not in old time by the will of man: but holy men of God spake as they were moved by the Holy Ghost" (2 Peter 1:20,21). The Greek word for "moved" is *phero*, meaning "to bring forth; to be driven; to move, rush." This sounds very much like the meaning of Jubal—the concept of bringing forth a stream, a rushing of waters. There is a related meaning, "to carry a burden." How similar this is to the Hebrew *massa*, which we know is the bearing of a burden, particularly the burden of a prophetic song. Holy men of God spoke as they felt the burden of the word given by the Spirit.

It must be noted and rememberd that the burden which comes is that given by the Spirit—not by oneself, or by fellow Christians, or by circumstances. Too often we find ourselves weighted down by a situation, and when a Scripture comes to mind, we think it is a prophecy. God's word comes from His origination, not from our reaction.

In our study on prophecy in chapter three of this book, we looked at the various tests that are to be applied to prophecy and the prophetic song. There is the test of the confirmation of the Spirit, but, as we noted then, this is the least reliable of the tests because our own spirit can be misled. We must never prophesy from what we feel or from the conclusions that we make about people or their circumstances. However, there is an inner prompting of the Spirit that we can recognize. There is a burden or a pressure within to speak forth what the Spirit gives. Perhaps a Scripture will be quickened and will burn within, and we "hear" it set to music in our spirit. Just because a melody or a set of lyrics comes to mind is not proof positive that it is the Spirit, because men are great improvisationalists; extemporaneous singing is not automatically the song of the Lord. But the burden of the Spirit confirms the song of the Spirit.

We do not go into a spiritual trance to receive the song of the Lord. Neither, as a rule, do we know the whole song before we sing it; we may know the beginning, but not the middle or the end until we are actually singing. It's like walking on the water: we have to get out of the boat and start to walk without knowing how far or how long we're going to walk. As we begin to sing the song, the middle and ending will come.

Prophecy comes forth by inspiration; therefore, faith is an essential ingredient. That inspiration is of God and comes from God. Without it the song will be natural, not spiritual. As we breathe in the Holy Spirit, we then can breathe out what He inspires. Perhaps that Divine inspiration will take the form of a heightened emotion, or a thought pattern that weighs upon the mind and spirit, which did not originate from our own thinking. We can be reasonably assured that that is the Spirit of God desiring to speak. But we should always check the source of our inspiration. Was it God, or was it someone or something to which we are reacting or responding?

As we lose ourselves in the presence of Jesus and release our spirits in praise and worship to Him, we find that He will put songs in our spirit. We do not consciously think of these songs or make them up ourselves; they are brought by the Spirit as Jesus is lifted up. We sing of the Lord's nature, name, and mighty acts. We extol Who He is. He becomes the essence of our song. "The LORD is my strength and song" (Psalm 118:14). He is the words and the music, the melody and the harmony. In His presence, as we see Him high and lifted up, we will be inspired to sing.

We have already seen in 2 Chronicles that "when the burnt offering began, the song of the LORD began also" (29:27). Our burnt offering today is ourselves and our praise. We offer our praise before God and it ascends as smoke from a burnt offering. We are to present ourselves "a living sacrifice, holy, acceptable unto God" (Romans 12:1). This kind of sacrifice brings pleasure to the Lord. "I will praise the name of God with a song, and will magnify him with thanksgiving. This also shall please the LORD better than an ox or bullock that hath horns and hoofs" (Psalm 69:30,31).

It is interesting to note that the prophetic song usually occurs in a service after the sacrifice of praise has taken place—that is, after a time (perhaps prolonged) of praising and singing new songs to the Lord—"singing in the Spirit," as some would call it. We need to remember that unless we are functioning in the office of a prophet or possess the gift of prophecy, we must not attempt to bring forth the prophetic song unless the spirit of prophecy is present; and if the spirit of prophecy is to be present, there must be praise and worship. Prophetic singing will not take place in a congregation that does not praise spontaneously, for God dwells in praises, and obviously if He is to speak, He must be present. Joy and rejoicing create the atmosphere in which the prophetic song may flow. It is unlikely that individuals would sing prophetic songs after the congregation had merely sung a few choruses and spent only a few moments praising. That's an insufficient atmosphere. As we offer the sacrifice of praise to God, the prophetic cloud comes.

The first prophetic song sometimes releases the spirit of prophecy so that others will also begin to step out and sing prophetically. We must not hold back or wait too long to step out and "break the ice" by singing the first prophetic song in a service. It is usually the first water out of the floodgates and is followed by much more water!

If we do not understand the prophetic song and have not been instructed in its nature and performance, we obviously will not flow easily in singing it. Few ever enter into something they do not understand, and without instruction they will not become skillful. There must be teaching, "line upon line, here a little, there a little." That is the reason why this book has been written and why it was thought of in the first place. We need to be taught the spiritual significance of the prophetic song and be aware of our ability and responsibility to enter into it. Today God wants believers who manifest the Divine through the prophetic song.

**Beginning the Prophetic Song**

At this point your question may be "How do I begin the prophetic song? How does it start?"

Usually the prophetic song begins with a melody. That melody may have begun on an instrument as the orchestra, the platform singers, and the congregation worship. When someone discerns that he has a melody or song of the Spirit, then when the praise diminishes in volume so that he can be heard, he should play out. Each musician should prefer his brother so that not all are playing at the same time or taking the song away from another by playing too loudly or changing the melody line. The musicians should let the melody line be firmly established before joining the song.

Once the melody is clearly stated, the words to the song may come through the same musician or through a singer or someone in the congregation. Whoever is singing should sing clearly and loudly (into a microphone, if possible) so that the words can be heard by everyone and be edifying to them. Perhaps the words can be written down and placed on the overhead projector; then the whole congregation can join in singing the song. Musically and lyrically, the song should be clear. It also should not be too long; if it becomes repetitious, that's an indication that the prophecy is complete. If there is a sense that the spiritual momentum of the song is diminishing, it is time to stop before the song of the Lord degenerates into the song of self.

Instrumentalists may play block chords or simple rhythms that supplement but do not take away from the dominant melody and the lyrics. That way every part complements the whole, and no one musician clamors for attention by playing complicated counter-melodies with a resultant cluttered sound. Chord progressions could develop with the established melody. The keyboardist should not force the singer to fit into his progression; he should follow. Chord progressions are often awkward because they manipulate the singer. The flow of the Spirit is restricted if the keyboardist and orchestra do not stop playing one chord progression when a new one begins. The musicians must be sensitive to changes that may happen musically when the prophetic song begins, and ask themselves if the song differs from what they have been playing.

The orchestra can color the picture the prophecy is painting by the way they play their instruments. We mentioned before the illustration of the instrument depicting falling water if the prophecy speaks of God coming as rain to His people. There are many other illustrations that could be given.

The song does not always begin on the instruments; sometimes it will start with a singer first and then move to the instruments. We must never try to establish a pattern or think that "this is the way to do it." We must allow God to be God. He is the Lord of the song, and He must do what He wants the way He wants to do it. Too often we go to praise and worship seminars and are told "how it should be done." That is a start, but please remember that God is on the Throne and we are in His Kingdom. We in our finite way are trying to teach God's ways, and at times we do miss the mark!

Preparation is so important—not just of oneself but of the surroundings. Everything in the physical environment—chairs, instruments, music stands, microphones, sound system, etc.— should be in order ahead of time. We know that David "prepared a place for the ark of God" (1 Chronicles 15:1). When all the natural things are in order, the minds of the people can be off the natural and on the spiritual. We certainly don't want the entire music department to be P.A.-conscious when they should be God-conscious!

This, of course, does not in any way lessen the importance of personal preparation. We've established that such preparation goes on all the time—not just five minutes before the service starts. However, a time of prayer prior to the service is very important. After a day in which our minds have been occupied with many other cares and concerns, we need a time in which to "tune in" to God and become aware of His Spirit. This can be a time of cleansing in preparation for ministry, and a time of making ourselves available to God and asking for His anointing. Just as athletes don't go on the playing field without preparation or warmup, we shouldn't just "show up" at the service and see what happens. We can't flow in the prophetic song if we're not ready. We need to be obedient to God when singing prophetically. God may want to say something that is different from what has been spoken or sung previously. Perhaps the song will be in a different style or rhythm than that which the congregation usually hears. (If it is a tremendous departure from the norm for that congregation, we do need to be doubly sure that the song is from God.) But obedience to the Spirit is a "must."

I challenge musicians to be creative and not always stick to the old and the familiar. Change the rhythm patterns and chord progressions if it is appropriate. Use your sanctified imagination to add your part to the song of the Lord. Be sensitive and complementary; ask God to give you something that will enhance.

Keep your eyes on the worship leader, choir director, or orchestra conductor. You may be asked to play more loudly or more softly, or to rest. They, too, are being sensitive to the Master Conductor. There is nothing wrong with the leadership conducting or directing the prophetic song as it unfolds. This does not take away from the spiritual quality of the song; it adds strength, beauty, and energy. For instance, when a singer is singing a soft prophetic song, the director or conductor can indicate how and when the violins or other instruments should accompany the song. This is true with the entire orchestra, even the percussionists or the brass section.

Congregational involvement in the prophetic song—as soon as possible after it begins—is important to eliminate the "spectator syndrome." Do not let the people merely watch as the musicians launch out into great depths of musical prophecy. This happens far too often because the congregation has not been taught about the prophetic song and their response to it. It also happens when the musicians get so lost in their singing or playing that they are unaware of what is happening in the congregation.

Singing is an advance. It is a spiritual march forward. So be bold! Sing out the words and melody God has given you. Let the voice of God be heard in the midst of His people. The enemy will try to counterattack by telling you that the song is not of God, or that you are singing to show off, or that it is not the right time to sing. That's why it is important to know that the song is of God by applying the tests we have discussed earlier.

Ask God to give you a new song. God delights in birthing new songs in His people. Ask in faith. Believe that it will happen as the Spirit moves. Prepare your heart and spirit. Make yourself available. Step out in faith and sing a new song unto the Lord! Then ask and expect Him to sing through you! It is exciting to sing new songs God gave other people, but it is even more exciting to sing a song God gives you.

It is awesome to listen to the song of the Lord—the prophetic song. You will never forget it once you've heard it. You will never be the same once you've sung it.

# Appendix

*Key Hebrew Words Suggesting Prophecy in Song*

1. Prophesy, Prophesied, Prophesieth, Prophesying(s), Prophet

   *Naba*: To speak or sing by inspiration (in prediction or simple discourse)

   Scriptures using *naba* with possible meaning of prophetic singing (*Strong's*, 5012):

   Numbers 11:25,26
   1 Samuel 10:11
   1 Kings 22:12
   1 Chronicles 25:1-3
   2 Chronicles 18:11
   Jeremiah 2:8
   Jeremiah 5:31
   Jeremiah 11:21
   Jeremiah 14:14-16
   Jeremiah 19:14
   Jeremiah 20:1,6

Jeremiah 23:16,21,25,26,32
Jeremiah 25:13,30
Jeremiah 26:9,11,12,18,20
Jeremiah 27:10,14-16
Jeremiah 28:6,8,9
Jeremiah 29:21,31
Jeremiah 32:3
Jeremiah 37:19
Ezekiel 4:7
Ezekiel 6:2
Ezekiel 11:4,13
Ezekiel 12:27
Ezekiel 13:22,16,17
Ezekiel 20:46
Ezekiel 21:2,9,14,28
Ezekiel 25:2
Ezekiel 28:21
Ezekiel 29:2
Ezekiel 30:2
Ezekiel 34:2
Ezekiel 35:2
Ezekiel 36:1,3,6
Ezekiel 37:4,7,9,12
Ezekiel 38:2,14,17
Ezekiel 39:1
Joel 2:28
Amos 2:12
Amos 3:8
Amos 7:12,13,15,16
Zechariah 13:3,4
Numbers 11:25-27
1 Samuel 10:5,6,10

1 Samuel 18:10
1 Samuel 19:20,21,23,24
1 Kings 18:29
1 Kings 22:8,10,18
2 Chronicles 18:7,9,27
2 Chronicles 20:37
Jeremiah 14:14 (prophet)
Jeremiah 23:13
Jeremiah 26:20 (prophet)
Ezekiel 13:17 (prophet)
Ezekiel 37:10
1 Samuel 10:13
1 Samuel 19:20
Jeremiah 29:26,27

2. Burden(s)

*Massa*: An utterance (often a doom), especially singing

Scriptures using *massa* suggesting that the "burden" was a prophetic song (*Strong's*, 4853):

Exodus 18:22
Exodus 23:5
Numbers 4:15,19,24,27,32,47,49
Numbers 11:11,17
Deuteronomy 1:12
2 Samuel 15:33
2 Samuel 19:35
2 Kings 5:17
2 Kings 8:9
2 Kings 9:25
2 Chronicles 24:27

2 Chronicles 35:3
Nehemiah 13:15,19
Job 7:20
Psalm 38:4
Isaiah 13:1
Isaiah 14:28
Isaiah 15:1
Isaiah 17:1
Isaiah 19:1
Isaiah 21:1,11,13
Isaiah 22:1,25
Isaiah 23:1
Isaiah 30:6
Isaiah 46:1,2
Jeremiah 17:21,22,24,27
Jeremiah 23:33,34,36,38
Ezekiel 12:10
Hosea 8:10
Nehemiah 1:1
Habakkuk 1:1
Zechariah 9:1
Zechariah 12:1
Malachi 1:1

### *Possible Prophetic Songs in the Bible*

(Prophetic in the sense that they are part of the inspired Word of God; that they are predictive or are *tehillah* praise)

1. Old Testament
    Exodus 15:1-19 . . . . . . . . The song of Moses
    Exodus 15:21 . . . . . . . . . . Miriam's song

Numbers 10:35,36 ......Songs of marching

Numbers 21:14,15 ......War songs

Numbers 21:17 ........Israel's song of the well

Numbers 21:27-30 ......War songs

Deuteronomy 32:1-43 ...The song of Moses

Judges 5:1-31 .........Deborah and Barak's song of thanksgiving

1 Samuel 2:1-10 .......Hannah's song of thankfulness

1 Samuel 18:7.........Song of the women of Israel about David and Saul

1 Samuel 21:11........A song of triumph

2 Samuel 1:17-27 ......David's lament over Saul and Jonathan

2 Samuel 3:33,34 ......David's lament of Abner

2 Samuel 22:1-51 ......David's song of victory

2 Samuel 23:1,2 ........A song of David

1 Kings 4:32 ..........1005 songs of Solomon

2 Kings 9:25 ..........The burden of King Joram

1 Chronicles 16:7-36 ....David's song of thanksgiving

2 Chronicles 20:14-19 ...A song of Jahaziel (possibly a prophecy in song—a prophecy of victory in battle)

2 Chronicles 20:21 ......A marching song

2 Chronicles 24:27 ......The burden of King Joash

2 Chronicles 29:27 ......Trumpeters playing the song of the Lord

Job 38:7 ..............The song of the morning stars

The book of Psalms .....150 prophetic songs. Possibly 73 sung by David; 11 by the sons of Korah; 12 by Asaph; 1 by Heman; 1 by Ethan; 2 by Solomon; 1 by Moses; 1 by Haggai; 1 by Zechariah; 1 by Ezra; an undetermined number by Hezekiah. The remaining authors are unknown.

Song of Solomon 1-8 ....A song of love by Solomon

Isaiah 5.1-8 ...........A prophetic song of the vineyard

Isaiah 12 ..............A song of praise

Isaiah 13:1-5 ..........A song of Babylon (possibly by Isaiah)

Isaiah 14:4 ...........A song of victory

Isaiah 14:28-32 ........Isaiah's song of Philistia

Isaiah 15:1-16:14 ......Isaiah's song concerning Moab

Isaiah 17:1-14 .........Isaiah's song of Damascus

Isaiah 19:1-25 .........Isaiah's song of Egypt

Isaiah 21:1-10 .........Isaiah's song of the fall of Babylon

Isaiah 21:11,12 ........Isaiah's song of Dumah

Isaiah 21:13-17 ........Isaiah's song of Arabia

Isaiah 22:1-14 .........Isaiah's song of the valley of vision

Isaiah 23:1-16 .........Isaiah's song of Tyre

Isaiah 26:1-11 .........Isaiah's song for the land of Judah

Isaiah 30:6,7 ..........Isaiah's song of the beasts of Negeb

Isaiah 35:10 ..........Songs of the redeemed

Isaiah 38:20 ..........Songs of Hezekiah

Isaiah 44:23 ..........The song of creation

Isaiah 54:1 ...........The song of the barren woman

Jeremiah 31:7,12 .......Songs of Israel

Lamentations 1-5 .......Jeremiah's song of Jerusalem (A series of dirges in the form of an acrostic, written as if for a national funeral)

Ezekiel 12:10-16........Ezekiel's song of the prince in Jerusalem

Jonah 2:9..............The song of Jonah

Nahum 1:1 . . . . . . . . . . . . The burden of Nineveh

Habakkuk 1:1-4 . . . . . . . . A song to God (possibly by Habakkuk)

Habakkuk 3:1-19 . . . . . . . A song of praise (possibly by Habakkuk)

Zephaniah 3:17 . . . . . . . . . A song of the Lord

Zechariah 9:1-9 . . . . . . . . Zechariah's song in the land of Damascus

Zechariah 12:1-14 . . . . . . Zechariah's song for Israel

Malachi 1:1-5 . . . . . . . . . . Malachi's song to Israel

2. New Testament

Luke 1:46-55 . . . . . . . . . . Mary's song of rejoicing

Luke 19:37 . . . . . . . . . . . . A song of high praise by the disciples (prophetic in the sense of proclaiming Jesus as King, for He was not yet King)

John 12:13 . . . . . . . . . . . . A song of high praise by a multitude of believers

Acts 2:2 . . . . . . . . . . . . . . The 120 disciples singing in the Spirit

Acts 16:25 . . . . . . . . . . . . Paul and Silas singing praises

Philippians 2:6-11 . . . . . . Congregation singing an early church hymn (possibly a new prophetic song when sung the first time)

1 Timothy 1:17 . . . . . . . . Congregation singing an early church hymn

1 Timothy 3:16 . . . . . . . . Congregation singing an early church hymn

Revelation 4:8 . . . . . . . . . Possibly a song sung by the Living Creatures

Revelation 4:10 . . . . . . . . Possibly a song sung by the twenty-four elders

Revelation 5:9,10 . . . . . . . A new song sung by the four Creatures and the twenty-four elders

Revelation 5:12 . . . . . . . . The song of millions of angels

Revelation 5:13 . . . . . . . . The song of all creation

Revelation 7:10 . . . . . . . . The song of the redeemed

Revelation 7:12 . . . . . . . . The song of the angels, the Living Creatures, and the elders

Revelation 14:3 . . . . . . . . The new song of the 144,000

Revelation 15:3 . . . . . . . . The song of the Lamb

Revelation 18:1,3,6-8 . . . . The song of the great multitude

# Bibliography

Blomgren, David K. *The Laying On of Hands and Prophecy of the Presbytery.* Portland, OR: Bible Press, 1979.

Blomgren, David K. *The Song of the Lord.* Portland, OR: Bible Press, 1978.

Conner, Kevin J. *The Tabernacle of David.* Portland, OR: Bible Press, 1976.

Cornwall, Judson. *Let Us Praise.* Plainfield, NJ: Logos International, 1973.

Harris, R. Laird. *Theological Wordbook of the Old Testament.* Chicago: Moody Press, 1980.

Hibbert, Mike and Vivian. *Music Ministry.* Hibbert, 1982.

*Interpreter's Dictionary of the Bible,* Volume 3. Nashville: Abingdon Press, 1962.

Manson, T. W. *Christian Worship: Studies in Its History and Meaning.* Oxford, 1936.

Martin, Ralph P. *Worship in the Early Church.* Grand Rapids, Michigan: William B. Eerdmans Publishing Company, 1964.

Philo. *Vit. Cont.*

Pick, Aaron. *Dictionary of Old Testament Words for English Readers.* Grand Rapids, Michigan: Kregel Publications, 1977.

Strong, James. *Strong's Exhaustive Concordance of the Bible.* McLean, VA: Macdonald Publishing Company, n.d.

# Endnotes

**Chapter 1:**
No references.

**Chapter 2:**
[1]Ralph Martin, *Worship in the Early Church* (William B. Eerdmans Publishing Company, 1964), page 13.
[2]Martin, page 13.
[3]T. W. Manson, *Christian Worship: Studies in Its History and Meaning.*
[4]Martin, page 40.
[5]Philo, *Vit. Cont.*, chapters 80 ff.
[6]Martin, page 41.
[7]Martin, page 47.

**Chapter 3:**
[1]Dr. David Blomgren, *The Laying On of Hands* (Bible Press, 1979).
[2]Blomgren, page 53.

**Chapter 4:**
[1]Dr. David Blomgren, *The Song of the Lord* (Bible Press, 1978), page 10.
[2]*The Interpreter's Dictionary of the Bible*, Volume 3 (Nashville: Abingdon Press, 1962), page 459.

**Chapter 5:**
No references.

**Chapter 6:**
[1]Mike and Vivian Hibbert, *Music Ministry* (1982), page 26.
[2]Hibbert, page 26.

# Resources from
# The Worship Institute

## The Worship Leaders' Training Course 1 & 2

*Becoming an effective worship leader takes more than music. This poweful resource series has touched hundreds of worship leaders around the country. LaMar Boschman and other leaders share how to prepare, empower, and increase your effectiveness as a worship leader. Available in audio or video with syllabus.*

## The Worship Team Training Course 1 - 3

*This unique course will equip and inspire your worship team. From playing together to praying together you will learn how to empower your worship team as never before. Seven leading worship ministers instruct you and your worship team. Each volume contains 4 - 45 minute videos.*

Plan now to attend the International Worship Institute. This five-day master worship intensive is held annually in Dallas/ Ft Worth and is attended by hundreds of worship ministers from around the world.

*For a free catalog, or more information contact:*

## *The Worship Institute*

*P.O. Box 130 ◆ Bedford, Texas 76095*

*www.worshipinstitute.com*

## *1-800-627-0923*

# Other Books
# By LaMar Boschman

### A Passion for His Presence

*Discover what the presence of God is and how to live in His presence daily.*

### Real Men Worship

*Learn how to be a real man who is a real worshiper.*

### Heart of Worship

*For those looking for worship revewal in their personal life as well as the local church.*

### Heart of Worship

*Explore the real meaning and purpose of music. Approximately 1,000 scriprures on music.*

*What will worship look like as we enter the next century? This book explores current worship trends and where they will take us in the future.*